Table of Contents

(continued on next page)

Table of Contents

Introduction

Collecting clocks can be rewarding, both personally and financially. Perhaps one of the greatest satisfactions clock collectors enjoy is knowing that their investments have practical as well as aesthetic value. Collectors can admire the beauty and craftsmanship of their clocks but also rely on them to keep them on schedule.

Another appeal of clocks is their universality and—pardon the pun—their timelessness. Clocks are universal because virtually everyone in our fast-paced society depends on them, and they are timeless because we have depended on the twenty-four hour time system for hundreds of years and will likely continue to do so far into the future. Thus, unlike other common household objects that have become obsolete, clocks will remain usable indefinitely, as long as they are kept in operable condition.

Quality antique clocks are an excellent investment because they hold their value. They aren't trendy. Well-made and maintained clocks will likely increase in value because they will never go out of style. They will provide useful service while they remain on display for owners and visitors alike to enjoy.

This guide is intended to be a user-friendly resource to help you quickly identify and estimate the value of a wide range of antique clocks. Have fun!

WITHDRAWN

Dan Brownell,
Editor

A Brief History of Clocks

The historical information and dates that follow present a succinct review of horological history. We have tried to show facts as accurately as our research permits; however, sources sometimes differ on dates, names, and other facts relevant to clock history.

885 Candles were used as clocks, an idea introduced by Alfred the Great of England.

1386 England's earliest known public clock was installed at the Salisbury Cathedral. It had no hands but told the time by striking on the hours.

1500 Peter Henlein of Nürnberg invented the mainspring.

1530 Screws for metal work became available.

Circa 1584 Galileo (1564-1642), an astronomer, physicist, and college professor, born in Pisa, Italy, was credited with discovering the properties of the pendulum. Galileo was a twenty-year-old college student (according to some sources, slightly younger) when on a visit to the city's cathedral, he watched a suspended lamp swinging to and fro. Timing it with the beat of his pulse, he discovered that a short swing moved slowly while a long one moved more rapidly. Because of this, each took the same amount of time to make a complete swing.

Early 1600s Pendulums with anchor or dead-beat escapement replaced the less accurate foliot balance.

Among the colonists who settled in 1607 and 1620 were skilled workers, including those with clock making knowledge. They made clocks one at a time, relying on England for their supplies.

1657 Dutch scientist Christiaan Huygens created the first pendulum based on Galileo's observations. The pendulum's back and forth swinging motion served as the clock's regulating mechanism.

1660 The balance or hairspring came into use.

1673 to 1771 George Graham's two essential contributions to clock making were the dead beat escapement and the mercurial compensation pendulum.

1680 Second hands made their first appearance.

1700 to 1799 Clocks appeared in homes as a mark of prosperity.

1715 A dead beat escapement for regulator clocks was invented.

1730 The German clock maker Anton Ketterer made his first cuckoo clock.

1759 Thomas Mudge of London invented the lever escapement.

1765 Pierre Le Roy of Paris made the first compensation balance.

1772 to 1852 Eli Terry became known as the father of the clock making industry.

Pre 1775 In colonial America, craftsmen made clocks to order, one at a time. This was an expensive, time-consuming process because brass movements were fashioned by hand with simple tools.

WITHDRAWN

Boston, New York, and Philadelphia were all centers for the production of the tall-case floor clocks, better known as grandfather clocks. During this time, several hundred clockmakers were at work in the colonies.

1775 to 1783 Clock making in the colonies came to a halt during the Revolutionary War as clockmakers joined the fighting forces or made equipment for the soldiers. Many clockmakers became gunsmiths.

1790 to 1812 Gideon Roberts, a Revolutionary War veteran, may have been the first to use mass production methods in his Bristol, Connecticut, clock factory where both hanging wall clocks and tall-case clocks were made. Many were sold to out-of-state buyers. Because brass clock works were expensive, he created his own wooden movements and used printed paper dials.

Some clocks were made without cases. Since their pendulums could be seen easily as they swung back and forth, the phrase "Wag-on-the-Wall" became an appropriate name for these clocks. Of course, a buyer could build a case or have a woodworker fashion one to make a conventional clock.

Roberts assembled his thirty-hour tall-case clocks with their wooden movements in groups of ten or more at a time. This innovation speeded up the production process and made less costly clocks available to buyers.

1793 Following the completion of his apprenticeship, Eli Terry began making clocks near Plymouth Hollow, Connecticut.

After 1800 Eli Terry learned how to use water power to drive machinery. This helped to increase the production of clock parts.

1802 Simon Willard patented his "improved timepiece," which was later called the "banjo clock" because of its shape. Originally, most examples were time only. Clockmakers have consistently copied this popular style over the years.

Eli Terry established his first factory.

1802 to 1840 Simon Willard made about four thousand clocks during this period. One model was the banjo clock, which sold for about $35.

Early nineteenth-century clock making was difficult because metal was scarce and the supply of glass was limited. All work had to be done by hand, and the craftsman and his apprentice used the simplest tools in their work: a hammer, drill, and file.

1807 to 1809 The Jefferson Embargo limited the importation of material from English factories.

1807 to 1810 Eli Terry contracted to make an unheard of four thousand hang-up clock movements at $4 each in three years. The water-power driven machines he designed produced identical interchangeable wooden parts for inexpensive (grandfather-type) clock works. Silas Hoadley and Seth Thomas worked for him. Terry is credited with introducing the factory system of mass production. This helped start the factory system in the United States. Inexpensive clocks, made in quantities, became available to the public.

1809 to 1810 Eli Terry established a partnership with Seth Thomas.

1810 to 1813 Seth Thomas and Silas Hoadley bought Eli Terry's Plymouth clock shop. Thomas sold out in 1813, and Hoadley continued in business.

1812 Eli Terry set up an experimental shop that produced low-priced wooden shelf clocks.

1813 Seth Thomas set up his own shop in Plymouth Hollow, Connecticut, where he became a prolific clockmaker.

1816 Eli Terry patented a pillar-and-scroll shelf clock with a thirty-hour wooden works that evolved from his plain box-type case. This clock cost about $15 and ran thirty hours on a single winding. For a short time, Chauncey Jerome made clock cases for Eli Terry.

Circa 1818 Joseph Ives made a brass clock movement with steel plates.

Seth Thomas and Eli Terry reached an agreement that Thomas was to pay Terry a royalty of 50 cents for each clock made. The agreement produced about five thousand clock movements.

1820 to 1840 Most of the Connecticut clock industry produced wooden shelf clocks. These clocks sold for less than $10. Brass clocks, on the other hand, ranged in price from $15 to $33 or more.

1824 Chauncey Jerome formed a partnership with his brother, Noble, and Elijah Darrow to manufacture clocks. The firm was called Jerome & Darrow, and was the largest producer of clocks at the time.

Joseph Ives perfected a spring-driven shelf clock using flat leafed springs instead of coiled ones.

Circa 1825 Jerome patented a "bronze looking-glass clock" with a thirty-hour wooden movement, bronze-colored pilasters, and a mirror instead of a tablet. Jerome specialized in case building and usually bought his movements from others.

Joseph Ives learned how to make rolled brass. He moved to Brooklyn, New York, where he stayed briefly, and invented the wagon spring to power a clock. The wagon spring is a series of flat-leafed arched springs that resemble those used in wagons.

1825 to 1920 "OG" or "ogee," S-curved, veneer-framed clocks were made and sold widely throughout this ninety-five-year period. They were prolonged best sellers.

1830 Eli Terry's son, Silas B. Terry, patented a method for tempering coiled springs so they could be produced inexpensively.

The spring balance was invented.

After 1830 Rolled brass became more available for clock movements.

1833 Eli Terry retired from active clock making.

1836 James S. Ives of Bristol, Connecticut, received a patent for a brass-coiled clock spring.

Circa 1840s Elias Ingraham, Bristol, designed a Gothic clock popularly called a "steeple" clock.

1840 Spring-driven clocks were introduced.

The largest clock factory was the Jerome Company owned by Chauncey Jerome.

1840 to 1842 Jerome sent a shipment of his brass clocks to England. When the first shipment arrived, English authorities realized that a very inexpensive and reliable clock was being imported and allowed them to be sold. English buyers purchased the entire lot. Jerome sent another lot, and the English bought all of these, too.

1840 to 1850 All American clocks were weight-driven until the mid-nineteenth century because the United States did not have rolling mills that were capable of producing spring steel.

1844 Brothers Elias and Andrew Ingraham formed a partnership with Elisha C. Brewster and started producing the steeple clock, which rapidly gained in popularity. This innovation soon replaced the large three-section Empire case, known as a "triple-decker," which was a popular item among Connecticut clockmakers of the 1830s.

1845 By this date, nearly a million clocks were being made in Connecticut each year.

1847 An economic depression stopped American clock making and ended the production of the wooden clock movement.

1849 The American Clock Company, New York City, was organized as a large depository to sell clocks made by various clockmakers. The company issued a catalog showing the clocks that were for sale.

1850 Spring-driven clocks gradually replaced weight-driven ones.

Anson Phelps established the Ansonia Clock Company in Ansonia, Connecticut.

Circa 1850 Brass-coiled springs were largely replaced by better and cheaper steel springs.

1850 to 1860 Tall-clock production came to a standstill.

Circa 1851 John H. Hawes of Ithaca, New York, patented the first known simple-mechanism calendar clock.

1859 Westminster chimes were introduced.

1864 Mozart, Beach & Hubbell patented a perpetual-calendar clock that needed to be wound only once a year.

1866 Plymouth Hollow was renamed Thomaston, Connecticut, to honor Seth Thomas. As a result, clock labels were changed to "Thomaston."

1867 A battery-operated clock was marketed.

1869 Celluloid, a flammable plastic, was developed. It was later used on clock cases to simulate tortoise shell, amber, onyx, and other materials.

1871 Daniel Gale of Sheboygan, Wisconsin, patented an astronomical calendar clock dial.

1880 H. J. Davis made an illuminated alarm clock.

1885 The Sidney Advertising Clock Company, Sidney, New York, developed a large wall clock on which advertising drums turned every five minutes.

1886 to 1916 The Darche Electric Clock Company, Chicago, Illinois, and Jersey City, New Jersey, made battery-alarm timepieces.

Circa 1888 The Self-Winding Clock Company, New York City, made electric and battery-powered clocks.

Late 1800s The Simplex Company of Gardner, Massachusetts, made time recorders and time clocks.

Leading Clock Manufacturers

The Ansonia Clock Company

Anson G. Phelps, a wealthy importer of tin, brass, and copper, founded the Ansonia Clock Company in 1850, six years after he built a copper rolling mill near Derby, Connecticut.

After a fire destroyed the factory in 1854, Phelps moved his company to a location he named Ansonia, and he renamed his business the Ansonia Brass and Copper Company. In 1878, shortly after moving clockmaking operations to Brooklyn, New York, a fire destroyed his factory. A year later, after building another factory, he expanded the business.

Ansonia was known for its diversity of clock types, including its models with "bobbing" and "swinging" dolls. The company's specialty clocks featured "swinging-arm" clocks, in which female figures held swinging pendulums. Also popular were Royal Bonn porcelain shelf models and statue clocks, which the company advertised as figure clocks. Among its novelty clocks, the Crystal Palace, Sonnet, Helmsmen, and Army and Navy models have proved to be excellent collector's items and have rapidly increased in value.

Just prior to World War I, Ansonia had sales representatives in a number of foreign countries. After the war, its business deteriorated and manufacturing ended in the spring of 1929. Later that year, the Russian government purchased the company's assets and, sadly, this creative clock manufacturer went out of business.

The William L. Gilbert Clock Company

George Marsh and William Lewis Gilbert purchased a clock shop in 1828, which they named Marsh, Gilbert & Company. In 1837, when John Birge joined Gilbert, the company name became Birge, Gilbert & Company. Then clockmakers Chauncey and Noble Jerome and Zelotas Grant became partners with Gilbert to create Chauncey Jerome's inexpensive brass movement clocks, and from 1839 to 1840, the company was known as Jerome, Grant, Gilbert & Company. In 1841, William Gilbert and Lucius Clarke acquired a clock factory in Winsted (later renamed Winchester), Connecticut.

From 1841 to 1845, Clarke, Gilbert & Company produced inexpensive brass clocks. In 1845, Gilbert bought Clarke's share in the company. Three years later, Clarke bought his shares back and the partnership lasted until 1851. The company was known as W. L. Gilbert & Company until 1866, when it became the Gilbert Manufacturing Company. Thirty years following its purchase in 1871, the Winsted (or Winchester) factory burned down, but Gilbert was not a quitter. He formed the William L. Gilbert Clock Company the same year. Gilbert died in 1890, but the company retained its name for the next sixty-three years.

George B. Owen managed the company from 1880 to about 1900. Despite financial problems from 1934 to 1957, the company remained active. During World War II, clock production was limited because the war effort required metal. However, the company was allowed to manufacture papier-mâché case alarm clocks rather than metal ones. These clocks enabled workers to get to their war-related jobs on time. After the General Computing Company took over the Gilbert Company, the name General-Gilbert Corporation was used. Unfortunately, by 1964, the company clock division was no longer profitable, and the Spartus Corporation purchased the company.

The E. Ingraham Company

Elias Ingraham (1805-1885) founded the E. Ingraham Company. He served a five-year apprenticeship with Daniel Dewey as a cabinet-maker. In 1828, he went to work for George Mitchell, a wise busi-nessman in Bristol, Connecticut. Mitchell wanted a worker who was creative and could produce new case styles. By succeeding in this task, Ingraham earned the reputation of being an innovative man in the clock industry. The exotic case he designed had mahogany columns, paw feet, turned rosettes, and carved baskets of fruit.

In 1830, Ingraham went to work for Chauncey and Lawson C. Ives to design cases for their clocks. One of his cases, a "triple-deck-er," could accommodate a long drop of weights. In the following three years, he made almost six thousand cases for the firm of Chauncey and Lawson C. Ives.

During the next ten years, Ingraham made clock cases, chairs, and mirrors. He helped design a Gothic case, named a steeple clock, which became extremely popular. These smaller clocks rapidly replaced the large Empire-style cases. In the mid-1840s, he formed a partnership with Brewster called Brewster and Ingraham.

The Ingraham Company, with its various name changes and part-ners, was one of the world's largest clockmakers. In 1855, the Ingraham factory in Bristol burned, resulting in a loss of about $30,000. Elias established a new firm when he made his son Edward a partner in 1857. The business name, E. Ingraham & Company, was used from 1861 to 1880. In 1881, the name was changed to The E. Ingraham & Company. This name stayed as such until 1884 when it became The E. Ingraham Company. During this period, the company manufactured clocks with black-painted or japanned cases. From 1914 to 1942, its products included non-jeweled pocket watches, wrist watches, eight-day lever movement clocks, electric clocks, and pendulum clocks. The company's clock making activities ended in 1967, when McGraw-Edison bought the company.

The New Haven Clock Company

In the early 1850s, the New Haven Clock Company was incorporated to produce inexpensive brass movements for the Jerome Manufacturing Company. When the Jerome company went bankrupt in the mid-1850s, the New Haven company purchased it. From then until the 1880s, the company did well. In addition to expanding its operations by making complete clocks, it promoted pocket watches and wrist watches. Through catalogs, New Haven sold its own clocks, as well as those made by the F. Kroeber Company of New York, the E. Howard Company of Boston, and E. Ingraham & Company of Bristol, Connecticut. New Haven soon became one of the largest clock companies in the United States. Among the clocks it produced were French clocks; jewelers' regulators; ebony and mahogany cabinet clocks; wall clocks, including calendar varieties; figure clocks (now called statue clocks); and tall-case hall clocks. In 1885, it stopped selling clocks manufactured by other domestic clock companies.

In the early 1880s, the company patented the novelty Flying Pendulum clock, which features a flying ball that takes the place of the pendulum. It was advertised as the best show-window attraction ever made, although it was not noted for its time-keeping accuracy. This unique clock has been reproduced from time to time, and as recently as the late 1950s.

By 1910, the company offered a vast range of clocks. From 1917 to 1956 the company was a major producer of inexpensive watches. A corporation, The New Haven Clock and Watch Company, took over the company in 1946, but financial woes plagued it from 1956 to 1959. After 107 years in business, the New Haven Clock Company's facilities and products were sold at a public auction in March 1960. One reason for the company's demise was its tremendous overproduction, which made it virtually impossible to make a profit.

The Seth Thomas Clock Company

Seth Thomas (1786-1859) became an apprentice in the cabinet-maker-joiner trade in the early 1800s. He worked with Silas Hoadley from about 1808 to 1810, under the supervision of Eli Terry near Waterbury, Connecticut. Terry needed help to fulfill a contract for four thousand hang-up wooden clocks, their movements, pendulums, dials, and hands. Thomas, a joiner, assembled the clocks using his wood-working techniques. All clocks were in running order when he finished.

In 1810, Thomas and Hoadley bought Terry's plant. They made tall-case clocks and thirty-hour clocks with wooden movements. Thomas sold his share of the business to Hoadley in 1813 and bought a shop in Plymouth Hollow, Connecticut, where he made tall-case clocks with wooden movements. This shop remained his workplace until 1853.

In 1839, Seth Thomas switched from using wooden to thirty-hour brass clock movements, and in about 1850, he began using springs rather than weights to power his clocks. By 1844, he had discontinued making wooden clocks. As a traditionalist, he was reluctant to change his clock making methods, but the change to brass-clock production was more profitable. Thomas' company was soon producing twenty thousand brass clocks annually. At the height of his brass-clock production, he built a brass rolling mill called the Thomas Manufacturing Company.

After Thomas' death in 1859, his three sons, Aaron, Edward, and Seth Jr., carried on the business, producing many new models of spring-driven clocks. Calendar clocks became an important part of their business as well. The residents of Plymouth Hollow respected Seth Thomas for the industries he established in the town. To show their appreciation, they renamed the town Thomaston six years after his death.

In 1879, Seth Thomas Sons & Company and the Seth Thomas Clock Company were consolidated. In 1931, the Seth Thomas Clock Company, established in 1853, became a division of General Time Corporation. Seth Thomas' great-grandson, Seth E. Thomas Jr., was chairman of the board until his death in 1932. The company's leadership passed out of the hands of the Thomas family and in 1970 became a division of Tally Industries.

The Waterbury Clock Company

The Waterbury Clock Company was a major clock producer in the United States from 1857 to 1944, a period of almost ninety years. It was originally started as a branch of the Benedict & Burnham Manufacturing Company, the largest brass producer in Waterbury, Connecticut. The company manufactured rolled and drawn brass, copper, cabinet hardware, and lamp burners.

The Waterbury Company was originally located in the Benedict & Burnham shops until it found larger quarters in Waterbury. Its growth was so rapid that by 1873 a large plant was built and expanded several times. By the late 1800s, Waterbury employed about three thousand people and made over twenty thousand watches and clocks daily. Waterbury became internationally known in the 1870s, when it had offices in Toronto and Glasgow.

Waterbury made and sold movements as well as complete clocks. By the turn of the century, it had a business relationship with Sears Roebuck, one of the big mail-order houses. Many styles of Waterbury clocks were sold, including eight-day time and strike models in oak cases, which sold for $2 each. In 1913, a Waterbury factory catalog illustrated over four hundred styles of clocks, starting at $1.20 each. Included were alarm, carriage, French mantel, and tall-clock models. In the early 1890s, it manufactured non-jeweled watches, including the famous dollar watch made for R. H. Ingersoll & Bros. It also acted as a selling agent for the Ithaca Calendar Clock Company. This latter affiliation lasted until 1891, when Waterbury introduced its own line of perpetual calendar clocks.

During the Great Depression in the 1930s, the company went into receivership, and its case shop and clock making materials and parts were sold at auction. Waterbury's life as a clock and watch manufacturer ended when the United States Time Corporation bought the company in 1944.

The E. N. Welch Manufacturing Company

Prior to 1831, Elisha Niles Welch (1809-1887) was in business with his father, George, who made weights and bells for clocks in an iron foundry in Bristol, Connecticut. When Elisha Welch formed a partnership with Thomas Barnes Jr., the company was called Barnes & Welch. They manufactured wooden movement shelf clocks. Barnes and

Welch were involved in business with Jonathan C. Brown and Chauncey Pomeroy.

From 1841 to 1849, E. N. Welch was a partner of J. C. Brown, who used the Forestville Manufacturing Company and J. C. Brown, Bristol, Connecticut, as company names. Chauncey Pomeroy was also a partner in these companies. They manufactured eight-day clocks with brass movements in the two factories. In 1853, fire destroyed J. C. Brown's Forestville Hardware and Clock Company. Welch bought Elisha Manross' failing clock parts business and J. C. Brown's Forestville Company, after it went bankrupt. He also purchased Frederick S. Otis' case-making business. He consolidated these purchases under one name, E. N. Welch, which became one of Bristol's largest clock companies.

In 1868, the Welch, Spring & Company was formed. It produced high-quality clocks, including regulator and calendar models. After Elisha Welch died in 1887, his son James became the company's president. Fire destroyed the movement factory in 1899. Later that same year, the case factory met the same fate. Financial problems plagued the company: Liabilities grew and legal suits were pending, but the company had no funds to meet its obligations. The Sessions family, which had a clock business in Forestville and wanted to expand, began buying Welch company stock. After Albert L. Sessions became treasurer and W. E. Sessions assumed the presidency, they borrowed over $50,000 to revitalize the company and changed the name to the Sessions Clock Company.

The Welch, Spring & Company

Elisha Niles Welch, Solomon Crosby Spring, and Benjamin Bennet Lewis organized Welch, Spring & Company. Their partnership lasted sixteen years, from 1868 to 1884. Each of these men had a talent that contributed to the success of the organization. Welch was the financier, Spring was the manager and design engineer, and Lewis was the inventor. The three men were interested in developing a superior quality clock line. This was contrary to the goals of other major clock companies in America that produced quantity rather than quality.

At 22, Welch formed a partnership with Thomas Barnes, using a Barnes and Welch label as their company's logo. On two separate occasions—in 1841 and again in 1880—he loaned money to J. C. Brown, a fellow clock maker. When Brown's company became insolvent, Welch purchased it and two other Bristol firms—The Forestville Hardware and Clock Company and The Frederick Otis Case Shop. He consolidated these clock holdings under the name of E. N. Welch Manufacturing Company. Because he was a wise and cautious investor, his projects always seemed to be successful. It was largely due to Welch's support that the Welch, Spring & Co. succeeded.

Lewis' contribution to the new company was his ability to develop calendar mechanisms, patenting three between 1862 and 1868. Spring was a renowned casemaker who specialized in rosewood cases. He learned basic techniques while working for the Atkins Clock Company. After leaving Atkins, he spent about twenty years operating his own business. Following his purchase of the defunct Birge, Peck and Company, he named it S. C. Spring Clock Company. This newly organized company supplied cases, movements, and parts to clockmakers in the Bristol, Connecticut area. He also manufactured vast numbers of clocks for the parent company.

Welch, Spring & Company passed through four stages in its sixteen years. The first stage, from 1868 to 1869, marked the period devoted to creating three standard shelf models—the Empress, the

Peerless, and the Italian. During the second stage, lasting from 1870 to 1876, emphasis was on the production of regulators and calendar clocks. The third stage, from 1877 to 1888, focused on selecting names for the company's clock models. Other manufacturers were using names of cities, rivers, and regents for their clock series. Spring and other staff members decided to name their clocks after popular artists in the opera and theater. The 1877 models were named Parepa, Lucca, Titiens, Verdi, Kellogg, Auber, and Wagner.

The fourth and final stage, called the Patti Era, lasted for five years, from 1879 to 1884. This developmental period was named for Adelina Patti (1843-1919), a Spanish coloratura soprano who won fame as one of the world's greatest operatic singers. Her career was almost without parallel in the history of the operatic stage. This period marked the company's final effort to be financially successful. The staff believed the company's success would depend on the success of the Patti model. Many considered the Patti the most collectible and famous parlor clock ever conceived by an American manufacturer. However, sales did not live up to expectations. The company tried to dress up the Patti to improve its sales. These changes, however, did not solve the company's problem. The demise of Welch, Spring & Company came because the clocks were too expensive for the general public. In 1884, the company ceased doing business. E.N. Welch purchased all of Welch, Spring & Company's buildings, inventory and machinery from his partners for $10,000. Despite this, E. N. Welch died a wealthy man in 1887, leaving an estate of approximately $3 million.

Advertising Clock

*Waterbury Long-Drop
Octagon Regulator
Advertising Clock, circa
1900, 4 1/2 x 17", 32"
high, $800-900*

Advertising clocks display
promotional information
on their cases, dials, or
tablets. Two early U.S
advertising clock compa-
nies began manufacturing
these wall clocks in the
late 1800s. The first was
the Sidney Advertiser
Company of Sidney, New
York; the second was the
Baird Company of
Plattsburgh, New York.
Baird's early clock cases
were made of papier-
mâché. Later, they were made of wood. Sidney featured a clock
with ads placed on a drum that turned every five minutes.

Annular Clock

*French Bronze Urn-Form
Annular Clock, circa 1895,
9 1/4" high, $4,592*

Annular means ring shaped.
Thus, these shelf clocks got
their name from their charac-
teristic construction, in which
the dial moves in a circle,
while the hand remains station-
ary, indicating the time as the
dial passes beneath it. Annular
clocks commonly have a single
hand, but some have two
hands, each pointing to a separate ring of numbers, one ring
displaying the hours, the other the minutes.

Banjo Clock

*Chelsea Clock Company
Mahogany-Case Banjo Clock,
circa 1933, 33" high, $1,120*

Simon Willard patented this wall clock in 1802. While he called it his "Improved Timepiece," it became known as the banjo clock because of its shape. It featured a pendulum that could be screwed down so the clock could be easily moved without damaging its suspension. Unlike many clocks of that day, the banjo clock is an original design rather than a version of a European clock. Although its popularity diminished after 1860, it has frequently been copied ever since.

Black Mantel/Temple-Style Clock

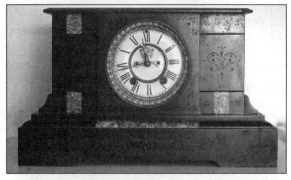

Ansonia Black Marble Temple-Style Clock, circa 1890, 7 x 17 1/2", 10 1/4" high, $400-450

"Blacks," or black mantel shelf clocks, were popular from about 1880 to 1920. Because black walnut was in short supply, these clocks were typically made of other black enameled wood, enameled cast iron, or black marble. They often had elaborate inlays, engravings, and brass ornamention. They were sometimes called "temple-style" when they resembled Greek temples.

Bracket Clock

Junghans Mahogany-and Poplar-Case Bracket Clock, circa 1915, 17 1/2" high, $532

Bracket clocks are sometimes mistakenly called mantel clocks because they look like they could sit on a shelf. However, they actually are designed to rest on a bracket attached to a wall. In addition, bracket clocks were produced about fifty years before mantel clocks. Being early models, bracket clocks were not mass produced. Rather, all parts were painstakingly made and assembled in a single shop.

Calendar Clock

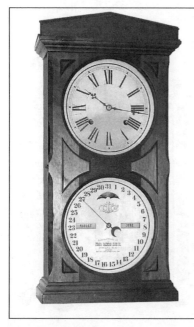

Ithaca "No. 10 Farmer's" Model Walnut-Case Calendar Clock, circa 1880, 24" high, $644

In about 1853, John Hawes of Ithaca, New York, made the first simple calendar clock in the U.S. Several years later, the first perpetual calendar clocks were produced. Perpetual calendar clocks are superior because they automatically adjust for leap years and differing numbers of days in the months. Most calendar clocks have two dials, one for time and the other for the date.

Carriage Clock

French Brass-Case Carriage Clock, circa 1920, 5 1/4" high, $218

Carriage clocks were designed to hang inside coaches, and were often covered with leather cases to protect them. They typically feature a rectangular brass case with glass front and sides, a porcelain dial, and a bail-type handle on top. Many also have a smaller subsidiary alarm dial below the main dial.

Cartel Clock

Charles Hour Louis XVI-Style Cartel Clock, circa 1900, 11 1/2" high, $392

Cartel clocks are carved wood or gilt metal wall clocks surrounded by very ornate decorations of ribbons, scrolls, leaves, and vines. The design was especially popular in France during the reign of Louis XVI.

Cottage Clock

*Jerome &
Company
Cottage
Clock, circa
1880,
13 1/2" high,
$364*

The cottage clock is a shelf model first made in the 1800s. It was popular until the beginning of the twentieth century. Most cottage clocks have 30-hour movements, wooden cases less than 12 inches high, and flat or three-sided tops.

Crystal Regulator Clock

Boston Clock Company "Crystal" Model Crystal Regulator Clock, circa 1890, 9 3/4" high, $560

Crystal regulators are shelf clocks so named because they typically have clear glass panels on all four sides, allowing their works to be seen. They are also known for being precise timekeepers.

Cuckoo Clock

*German Black Forest
Carved Hardwood
Cuckoo Clock, probably
post-World War II,
13 1/2 x 15", 23" high,
plus chains, $200-250*

Cuckoo clocks, which
originated in the Black
Forest of Germany in the
1700s, are wall clocks
that usually have ornately
carved wooden cases in
the shape of a house or
cottage and are decorat-
ed with birds and foliage.
On some models, when
the clock strikes the
hour, a bird pops out
from behind a door,
chirping the number of
times that corresponds to the time.

Gallery Clock

Empire Clock Company 1930s Oak-Frame
Gallery Clock, circa 1930, 16" diameter, $123

Gallery clocks, first introduced in 1845, have large round dials printed with large, dark numbers so they can be easily read from a distance, which made them ideal for use in train stations, lobbies, and other large public gathering places. They generally have plain cases with narrow borders to lend aesthetic balance to the over-sized dials.

Glass-Dome Clock

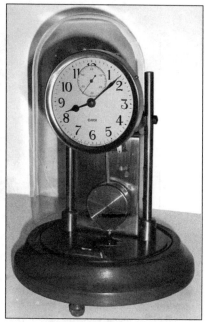

Barr Manufacturing Company "Executive" Model Glass-Dome Clock, circa 1920, 11" high, $364

Glass-dome clocks, like crystal regulators, expose their works to view. The domes are most often tall and narrow and are seated on circular wooden bases. The domes are especially effective in protecting the clocks because they provide an airtight seal against dust that could collect on the works.

Gothic/Beehive Clock

Brewster & Ingraham Rosewood-Case Gothic/Beehive Clock, circa 1845, 19" high, $560

Gothic clocks are so named because their shape incorporates the classic gothic arch. They are also known as "beehive" clocks because they also resemble the gently curving cone shape of a beehive. These clocks were widely produced by most U.S. clock manufacturers from the 1840s until the early 1900s.

Grandfather Clock

*Colonial Manufacturing Company
Queen Anne Revival Mahogany-
Case Grandfather Clock, circa 1919,
87" high, $1,512*

Grandfather clocks, also known as hall, tall, floor, or long-case clocks, are weight-driven clocks first made in England in the 1660s. They were among the most common early clocks in the colonies because the settlers did not yet have mills capable of producing springs for spring-driven clocks. Grandfathers were large because they required a tall case to provide an adequate drop for the weight to power the clock. Those made in the colonies were copies of English styles.

Lantern Clock

English Lantern Clock, circa 1890, 15 1/2" high, $1,624

Lantern clocks were first produced in England and follow a Gothic design. Their frames and sides are made primarily of brass with a dial that overlaps the front. The top forms an arch that makes it resemble a hand-held lantern.

Mantel-Garniture Clock

French Mantel-Garniture Clock Set, circa 1880, eight-day movement, time and strike, clock 5 1/2 x 9", 15 1/2" high, the set $1,400-1,500

Mantel garniture sets incorporate ornate clocks and accompanying pairs of urns, candelabra, or statues. They were most popular at the beginning of the twentieth century and were produced primarily in France.

Metal-Front/Metal-Case Clock

French Silvered Bronze-Case Clock, circa 1890, 10 3/4" high, $560

Metal-front and metal-case clocks became more common in the U.S. after the mid-1850s as more foundries opened. Until then, wood had been the primary material for clock cases and works. Metal cases were commonly molded with elaborate designs and then painted or gilded.

Mirror Clock

Jerome & Darrow Classical-Style Painted-Wood Case Mirror Clock, circa 1830, 33 1/2" high, $364

The mirror clock had a "looking glass" that replaced the usual picture or design, which made it popular among thrifty housewives who liked its dual purpose. The mirror clock enjoyed its heyday during the American Empire Period, from 1825 to 1840.

Novelty Clock

*New Haven Clock Company "Hickory
Dickory Dock" Model Novelty Clock, circa
1910, 43" high, $2,240*

Novelty clocks have unusual features specifi-
cally designed to entertain. Ansonia was one
of the first manufacturers to produce novelty
clocks, patenting the swinging and bobbing
doll models in the 1850s. In the 1880s, the
New Haven Clock Company produced the
Flying Pendulum Clock, considered one of
the most creative novelty clocks ever made.
Other major novelty clock manufacturers
include Lux and Keebler.

Octagon Clock

New Haven Clock Company "No. 2 Office Regulator" Model Octagon Clock, circa 1880, 41" high, $1,400

Octagon clocks were often referred to as "schoolhouse clocks," but they were also used in large workplaces and factories to keep employees informed of the time. They are classified as short drop or long drop, depending on the length of the case. They were most common from the mid-1800s to the early 1900s.

OG (Ogee) Clock

Alden A. Atkins Mahogany-Veneer OG-Case Clock, circa 1845, 26 1/2" high, $280

An OG clock is one that has an ogee, or S-shaped molding, around the door of its box frame. It typically has a decorated tablet, and early models were over two feet tall to accommodate their weight-driven movements. OGs were best sellers for nearly a hundred years, from 1825 to 1920.

Parlor Clock

*F. Kroeber Clock Company
"Langtry" Model Walnut-
Case Parlor Clock, circa
1870, 22 3/4" high, $672*

Parlor clocks are products
of the Victorian era.
Reflecting the formal style
of this mid-to-late 1800s
period, they were elegant
in design and intended to
be displayed on a shelf or
mantel in a family's parlor,
typically the best room in
the house, where guests
were entertained. These
clocks often have carved
walnut cases and stenciled
glass doors.

Pillar-and-Scroll Clock

Seth Thomas Federal-Style Mahogany-Case Pillar-and-Scroll Clock, circa 1825, tablet with paint loss, 31 1/2" high, $2,415

Eli Terry, considered "The Father of the Clock Making Industry," created the pillar-and-scroll design in about 1816. It was probably America's first mass-produced clock. The case characteristically has a scroll-cut top with three urn-form finials, a slender pillar on each side, and a reverse-painted glass tablet below the dial.

Porcelain/China Clock

Ansonia Clock with Royal Bonn China Case, circa 1900, minor imperfections, 15" high, $1,320

Porcelain/china clocks have cases made of glazed ceramic. Although the Royal Bonn Company of Germany made many of these colorful handpainted cases with French or rococo sashes, the Ansonia Clock Company made most of the works.

Pressed Oak Clock

E. Ingraham Commemorative Pressed Oak Clock 1898, eight-day movement, time and strike, 4 1/4 x 14 1/4", 23" high, $2,000-2,500

Inexpensive oak kitchen clocks were produced in large numbers from the late 1800s to about 1915. Their pressed designs were created with a rotary press that forced the design into the wood after steam had softened it. The clocks also featured glass panels decorated with bronze or silver gilt.

Statue/Figural Clock

French Cast-Bronze Figural Clock with Hunting Scene, late nineteenth century, $3,850

Figural clocks, now known as statue clocks, feature representations of people, animals, or mythical beings. Internationally, France was the most significant manufacturer of these clocks. Within the United States, the Ansonia Clock Company was the early leader.

Steeple Clock

E.C. Brewster Mahogany-Veneer-Case Steeple Clock, circa 1855, 19 1/2" high, $448

In the 1840s, Elias Ingraham created this clock with a pointed Gothic-style "roof," two or four spires, and decorated glass tablet. The clocks used the newly developed brass springs and were tremendously popular. In fact, they are still made today.

Swinging-Arm Clock

French Patinated-Metal Swinging-Arm Clock, late nineteenth to early twentieth century, $1,955

A swinging-arm clock is one in which a figure, often a classical maiden, holds aloft a swinging pendulum. The top of the pendulum holds the clock, while the bob at the bottom helps regulate the time. Swinging-arm clocks were made to be displayed in jewelry store windows to capture the attention of potential customers.

Tambour Clock

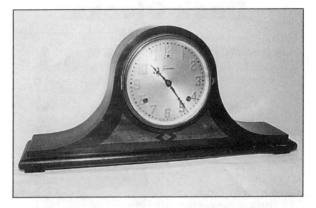

Sessions "Dulciana" Model Mahogany Tambour Clock 21 1/2" wide, 10" high, $175

The tambour clock is also known as a humpback or camelback clock because of the distinctive shape of its case, which is round in the center with sides that gently slope away and flatten. The style, introduced at the beginning of the twentieth century, has remained popular and is still being produced today.

Two- and Three-Deck Clocks

Atkins & Downs Mahogany-Case Two-Deck Clock, circa 1832, 39 1/2" high, $1,344

In the 1830s, during the American Empire Period, Elias Ingraham invented the three-deck, or triple-decker clock. Its tall case accommodated the drop needed for a weight-driven clock, as the springs required for a spring-driven clock could not yet be manufactured in the United States. Within fifteen years, smaller clock cases became more popular, and the production of two- and three-deck clocks began to wane.

Birge, Mallory & Company Classical-Style Mahogany-Veneer Three-Deck Clock 5 x 17 1/2", 38 3/4" high, $1,500-1,700

Wag-on-the-Wall Clock

French Morbier "Two-Weight Prayer" Model Pressed-Brass Wag-on-the-Wall Clock, circa 1890, 54" high, $672

This clock gets its name because it doesn't have a case to enclose the pendulum. Thus, the pendulum is completely exposed as it swings back and forth. In the U.S., early clocks were sometimes made without cases to make the works easier and cheaper to transport over long distances. While the owner had the essential parts needed to keep the time, once he arrived at his destination, he had the option to have a case built to make a conventional clock.

Wall Regulator Clock

Waterbury Clock Company "Regulator No. 82" Model Mahogany-Case Wall Regulator Clock, circa 1914, 41" high, $1,120

A regulator is a clock with exceptional accuracy, made possible by the invention of the deadbeat escapement in 1715. Regulators were called such because their accuracy allowed them to be used for regulation of less accurate clocks and watches. In fact, they were used in train stations and jewelry stores, where great accuracy was essential. Over time, however, less accurate clocks were labeled regulators, so eventually the term "regulator" just became a generic name for a hanging wall clock.

Advertising Clocks

Baird Eight-Day Spring-Driven Advertising Clock

Baird: Advertising wall clock, ca. 1896, eight-day, time only, spring driven, 31" h. **$1,500**

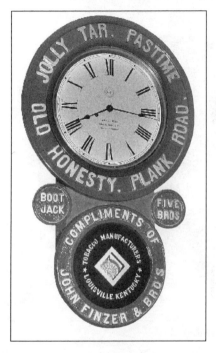

Baird Papier-Mâché-Case Advertising Clock

Baird: Papier-mâché-case wall clock, w/movement by Seth Thomas, ca. 1890, eight-day, time only, spring driven, 18 1/2" w., 30 1/2" h. $1,500

Bulova Electric Advertising Clock

Bulova: Electric wall clock, 16" d. **$110**

Coca-Cola Electric Advertising Clock

Coca-Cola: Electric wall clock, 16" w., 16" h. $90

W.L. Gilbert Eight-Day Spring-Driven Advertising Clock

Gilbert, W.L.: Dark-stained wall clock advertising Sauer's Extracts, glass etched, coins are gold leafed, eight-day, time only, spring driven, 40" h.................**$2,750**

L. Hubbell Birdseye-Maple-Case Advertising Clock

Hubbell, L.: Birdseye-maple advertising shelf clock, ca. 1870, eight-day, time only, 10 1/2" w., 24" h. **$2,500**

*E. Ingraham
Time-Only
Advertising
Clock*

Ingraham, E.: Wall clock advertising Ever-Ready Safety Razor, time only, 18" d., 29" h. **$4,000**

E. Ingraham Oak-Case Advertising clock

Ingraham, E.: Oak simple calendar clock, "Josephson, the Quality Jewelry Store" on lower tablet, eight-day, time only, spring driven, 11" d. dial, 16" w., 36" h., ...$450

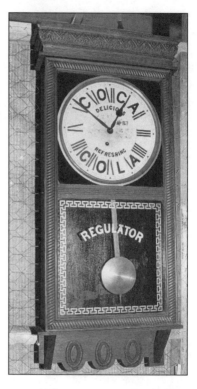

E. Ingraham Oak-Case Advertising Clock

Ingraham, E.: Oak advertising wall clock, ca. 1900, "Coca Cola, Delicious, Refreshing" on dial, eight-day, time only, 17" w., 38" h. $450

*Sessions Walnut-Case
Jeweler's Regulator
Advertising Clock*

Sessions: Walnut jeweler's regulator wall clock, 1902, advertising Weiler's Music Store, Quincy, Illinois, time only, 38 1/2" h. **$650**

Sessions Walnut-Stained-Case Advertising Clock

Sessions: Walnut-stained La Reforma advertising wall clock w/repainted tablet, ca. 1903, eight-day, time only, spring driven, 16 1/2" w., 38" h. **$595**

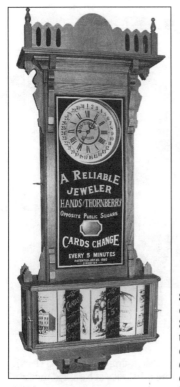

Sidney Oak-Case Calendar Advertising Clock

Sidney: Oak calendar wall clock, w/movement by Seth Thomas, repainted tablet & replaced exact copies of advertising drums, eight-day, time only, spring driven, 28" w., 72" h...................**$9,000**

*Waterbury
"Orient" Model
Short-Drop
Jeweler's
Advertising Clock*

Waterbury: "Orient" square-top, short-drop jeweler's wall clock, eight-day, time only, spring driven, 10" wide at base, 15" wide at top, 9" d. dial, 27" h...**$550**

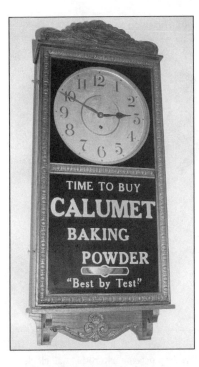

Waterbury Oak-Case Advertising Clock

Waterbury: Oak advertising wall clock, "Calumet Baking Powder," repainted tablet, eight-day, time only, spring driven, 16" w., 38" h. **$595**

*Waterbury
Reverse Dial Oak-
Case Short-Drop
Octagonal
Advertising Clock*

Waterbury: Oak-case short-drop octagon advertising wall clock w/reversed dial & hands that turn counterclockwise, often used in barbershops to reflect time in mirror, eight-day, time only, spring driven, 11" d. dial, 23" h. **$800**

Annular Clocks

French Alarm-Type Annular Clock with Flat-Topped Milk-Glass Globe and Cylindrical Brass Base

France: Night clock, alarm-type, a flat-topped milk-glass globe w/Roman numerals around center indicating the time, smaller Arabic numerals low on the globe for alarm, a short ringed neck holds the globe above a cylindrical brass base w/embossed scroll band around the middle, flaring base w/short feet, 30-hour pendulum-driven movement, bell present inside case, alarm set hand stuck to main drive w/dried grease, alarm winder missing, ca. 1890, 6" h...**$616**

French Louis XVI-Style Annular Clock with Ovoid Milk-Glass Chimney, Crown-Like Finial and Ornate Gilt-Spelter Base

France: Night clock, Louis XVI-style case topped by a pierced gilt-spelter crown-like finial over an/ovoid milk-glass chimney w/pink band at top & pink scalloped design at base, white middle panel w/black Arabic numerals, waisted ring-turned neck connects globe to ornate gilt-spelter base w/applied swags, notching, ribbing & high scroll feet, large cut-out hand indicating time, 30-hour time-only pendulette movement, ca. 1890, 13" h. **$2,016**

French "Temple de l'Amour" Model Annular Clock with Domed Top, Green Marble Columns, Cross-Legged Figure and White Marble Stand

France: "Temple de l'Amour," Louis XVI period, ormolu domical top w/finial, set within four ringed knob-topped columns connected w/ropetwist swags, an arrow suspended between the swags pointing to the black numerals on the white number panels just under the dome, the escapement visible below them, all on a white marble stand w/ormolu gallery, bead border w/chain swags, the top section supported by four green marble columns w/ormolu capitals & bases connecting it to the round white marble w/ormolu bead border & short tapering feet, centered between the columns is an ormolu figure sitting cross-legged on a drum-like pedestal holding a parasol, the movement planted in the case horizontally, the escape wheel driven through a contrate wheel & released by a conventional verge & pendulum, ca. 1790, 17" h. **$14,000**

*Japy Louis XVI-Style
Annular Clock with
Ornate Gilt-Bronze Urn
with Scrolling Handles
and Finial on Gilt-Bronze
Base with Painted Panels
and Coiled Serpent*

Japy (France): Louis XVI-style, the hour & minute panels w/white number cartouches run around a large ornately decorated gilt-bronze urn w/finial & scrolling handles sitting atop the rectangular gilt-bronze base w/beveled top supporting a serpent that coils around & up the base of the urn, its tongue pointing to the time, each side of the base inset w/an oval Sevres porcelain panel painted w/floral sprays in brilliant colors, short pendulum, time-only movement w/suspension spring, a driveshaft ascends from the movement up the stem of the urn & drives the minute & hour dials, w/Medaille D'Or trademark, ca. 1860, 15" h. $7,840

Night-Clock-Style Metal-Case Annular Clock in Form of a Lighthouse with a Spired Dome Top and Incised Bricks on Molded Base

Night clock: Patinated metal case in the form of a lighthouse w/a spired domed top over slender baluster-form colonettes flanking the annular-style cylindrical white dial w/black Arabic numerals, the cylindrical body w/incised "bricks" & applied doors & windows on molded base, time movement in base, a driveshaft up the tower turning a ventilated base plate that holds the lens, ca. 1880,
21 1/2" h. **$2,800**

Swiss Annular Clock with Silver Egg-Shaped Case, Hand-Painted Cameos, Chain Swag, and Octagonal Marble Base

Switzerland: Opalescent yellow enamel over damascene-patterned silver egg-shaped case, the top w/patterned finial & three h.p. cameos ranged around it & gold border w/scalloped design, number panels directly below, chain decoration swagged under number panels & partially framing h.p. front cameo of woman w/needlework, the top of the swag pointing to the time, on scalloped stem in same pattern as finial, ringed circular base, all on a white marble octagonal base, gold over silver hardware, time-only movement, some oxidation to gold, minor losses to marble base, ca. 1870, 7 1/4" h...$4,200

Swiss Sundial-Style Annular Clock with Brass Molded Case and Gnomon Pointing to Dials in Cut-Out Section on Top

Switzerland: Sundial-style, stepped brass circular molded case w/pierced scroll design gnomon on top, incised scrolling designs on either side of gnomon & on one tier of body, gnomon pointing to silvered metal annular dials that are revealed in cut-out section of top, Roman numerals for time & Arabic numerals for date, eight-day jeweled lever movement, bottom-wound & set, ca. 1955, 3 1/2" h. **$560**

Banjo Clocks

*Ansonia "Girandole"-Style
Mahogany Case Banjo Clock*

Ansonia: "Girandole" mahogany banjo wall clock w/Westminster chimes, brass sidearms, & cut glass on throat & on round beveled glass door at base, eight-day, time & strike, spring driven, 12" d. at base, 8" d. dial, 39" h. **$2,500**

Chelsea Walnut-Case Banjo Clock

Chelsea: Walnut banjo clock, ca. 1890, time only, single weight driven, made in Boston, 39" h...**$3,500**

*Howard & Davis "No. 3"
Model Cherry-Case Banjo
Clock*

Howard & Davis: "No. 3"
model, molded grained
cherry case, round top
around the dial w/black
Roman numerals, center &
bottom panels reverse-
painted in black w/gilt highlights, bottom panel w/oval
center for viewing pendu-
lum, time-only signed movement, lower baffle board &
tie-down missing, weight
incorrect, some gold loss to
lower tablet, ca. 1855,
38" h.......................**$3,360**

*E. Howard & Company
Rosewood-Case Banjo Clock*

Howard, E. & Company:
Rosewood rounded-end box
banjo wall clock, ca. 1840,
eight-day, time only, 11" w. at
base, 7" d. dial, 28 1/2" h. **$1,800**

E. Ingraham & Company
"Nyanza" Model Revival-Style
Banjo Clock with Walnut Case

Ingraham, E. & Company:
"Nyanza" model revival-style banjo
wall clock, walnut case w/pointed
ball finial atop the round dial
w/Arabic numerals above the slender tapering neck w/a reverse-
painted glass panel over the bottom pendulum box reverse-painted
in black w/a narrow gold-bordered
window to show the pendulum
bob, tapering concave bottom
drop, copy of an early 19th c.
model, ca. 1920, 4 1/2 x 10 1/8",
39" h.....................................**$450**

Massachusetts Weight-Driven Mahogany-Case Banjo Clock

Massachusetts: Weight-driven, mahogany case w/clean geometric lines & crotch mahogany panels in neck & large bottom rectangular door, original dial w/Roman numerals, pendulum & weight, time-only movement, ca. 1840, 29 1/2" h. $1,400

Sessions Clock Company
Mahogany-Finished Banjo Clock

Sessions Clock Company:
Mahogany finished banjo wall clock
w/Sessions on dial, eight-day, time
& strike, 6" d. dial, 10 1/2" w.,
35" h. $275

*Elmer Stennes
Mahogany-Case Ribbon-
Stripe Banjo Clock*

Stennes, Elmer: Mahogany
ribbon stripe banjo clock,
marked MCIP (made
clock in prison), one
weight, time only, 7" d.
dial, 44" h.. ....**$2,750**

Seth Thomas Clock Company "Danvers" Model Inlaid-Mahogany-Case Banjo Clock

Thomas, Seth, Clock Company: "Danvers" model, inlaid mahogany case, the top round molded frame w/a cast gilt-metal spread-winged eagle finial above the brass bezel enclosing the steel dial w/Arabic numerals, the tapering case & neck flanked by brass scrolls, rectangular base w/contour tapering base drop, eight-day four-jewel lever movement, part of label remains, some crazing, ca. 1930, 18 3/4" h. **$134**

Black Mantel/ Temple-Style Clocks

Ansonia Black Mantel Clock with Polished Mahogany Case

Ansonia: "Cabinet Antique" polished mahogany cabinet clock w/antique brass trimmings, French sash, finials, porcelain & brass face, eight-day, time & strike, 9 1/4" w., 20" h..........$2,750

Ansonia "The Senator" Model Black Mantel Clock

Ansonia: "The Senator" polished mahogany cabinet clock, antique brass trimmings, silver dial, eight-day, time & half-hour gong strike, 19" w., 22" h. **$4,000**

Ansonia "Cabinet Antique No. 1" Model Black Mantel Clock

Ansonia: "Cabinet Antique No. 1" polished mahogany shelf clock, ca. 1896, antique brass trimmings, porcelain & brass dial, eight-day, time & half-hour, Old English bell strike, 11 1/2" w., 18 3/4" h..$3,750

Ansonia Temple-Style Clock with Black-Painted Iron Case

Ansonia: Black-painted iron temple-style case, a flat rectangular top above a large brass bezel enclosing the dial w/Roman numerals, incised gilt scrolls at corners, deep-stepped base w/further incised gilt scrolls, gilt-metal scroll & paw feet & lion head masks at the ends, eight-day movement, time & strike, ca. 1900, 5 3/4 x 10 1/4", 12 1/4" h. $300-350

Ansonia Temple-Style Clock with Black-Finished Iron Case

Ansonia: Black-finished iron temple-style case, the flat rectangular top above a wide ornate brass bezel w/beveled glass around the dial w/Arabic numerals & a raised central gilt-brass center ring, gilt-trimmed incised sprigs flank the dial, the thick platform base w/further gilt sprigs, eight-day movement, time & strike, ca. 1900, 6 x 9", 10 1/2" h. **$300-350**

Ansonia "Capri" Model Temple-Style Clock with Cast-Iron Black Enameled Case

Ansonia: "Capri" cast-iron, black-enameled mantel clock, ca. 1890, porcelain dial, open escapement, eight-day, time & strike, 15" w., 12" h. **$350**

Ansonia Temple-Style Clock with Cast-Iron Black Enameled Case

Ansonia: Cast-iron, black-enameled mantel clock, slate dial, open escapement, four marbleized columns & trim, ca. 1890, eight-day, time & strike, 16" w., 13" h. **$500**

W.L. Gilbert "Curfew" Model Italian-Marble-Finish Black Mantel Clock

Gilbert, W.L.: "Curfew" Italian-marble-finish mantel clock, ca. 1910, eight-day, time & strike, 16" w., 17 1/2" h. **$375**

Ingraham Company Temple-Style Clock with Black Enamel Over Wood Case

Ingraham Company: Temple-style, black enamel over wood, the long, high rectangular case w/applied stamped-metal columns & cast-metal paw feet, metal lion-head mask end handles, top panels on the front inset w/slag glass framed by metal simulating curtained windows, eight-day movement, time & strike, ca. 1900, 5 1/2 x 20", 10 7/8" h. $300-400

F. Kroeber Black Mantel Clock with Cast-Iron Black-Enameled Case

Kroeber, F.: Cast-iron black-enameled mantel clock, ca. 1898, gilded decorations, eight-day, time & strike, 12 1/2" h. **$275**

Sessions Temple-Style Clock with Cast-Iron Black Enameled Case

Sessions: Cast-iron black-enameled mantel clock, gilded decorations & feet, eight-day time & strike, 15" w., 10" h. **$175**

Waterbury Temple-Style Clock with Black-Painted Wood Case

Waterbury: Black-painted wood temple-style case, flat rectangular top above the projecting central section w/an ornate brass bezel enclosing the dial w/Roman numerals, small creamy celluloid column w/gilt-metal capitals & bases at each side, deep stepped base w/rounded corners, raised on scrolling gilt-metal feet, eight-day movement, time & strike, ca. 1900, 7 1/4 x 15 1/2", 10 5/8" h.
....**$200-250**

*Waterbury
Iron-Front
Black
Mantel
Clock*

Waterbury: Iron-front black-shelf clock w/floral & gilded decorations, ca. 1850, 30-hour, time & strike, spring driven, 3 1/2" d. dial, 12" w., 16" h...**$200**

Waterbury Black Mantel Clock with Cast-Iron Black Enameled Case

Waterbury: Cast-iron black enameled mantel clock, brass dial, brass-applied decorations, eight-day, time & strike, 9 1/2" w., 11" h. **$275**

Bracket Clocks

English Greek-Style Mahogany-Case Bracket Clock with Arched Beveled Top

England: Greek-style mahogany case w/arched beveled top over molded pediment, molding & inlay decoration all around w/fret side panels, three-quarter round ring-turned columns flanking glassed arch-shaped door, molded-top block base on rectangular wafer feet, the arched silvered metal dial w/engraved brass decoration, Arabic numerals & strike/silent, tune selection & F/S subsidiary dials, eight-day triple fusee movement, clock chimes on eight bells or five gong rods w/choice of Whittington or Westminster tune, made for Theodore B. Starr & Co., small sliver of wood missing from rear, very minor dry splits in veneer, ca. 1910, 18 1/2" h. **$3,584**

English Mahogany-Case Bracket Clock with Molded Ogee Top

England: Mahogany rectangular case w/molded ogee top w/ormolu swag decoration on front, center urn-form finial & four similar corner finials, the arched ormolu dial panel w/silvered metal chapter ring in round time dial w/Roman numerals & in three subsidiary dials ranged above it, the body accented w/ormolu caryatids at the corners & broad acanthus moldings around waist, heavy cast sound frets & folding handles at the sides, three-fusee double chime time & strike movement, chimes the quarters on a choice of eight bells or four gongs, strikes the hours on a fifth large gong, some dry splits in front of case, ca. 1890, 27 1/2" h. **$5,320**

Franz Hermlie Music Box Bracket Clock with Stained Fruitwood Case

Hermlie, Franz (Germany): Music box clock, stained fruitwood case w/a domed, stepped top w/bail handle, square front door opening to a brass & enamel dial w/Roman numerals, pairs of knob-turned spindles on each side, platform base w/flat feet, eight-day time & strike movement, 8 1/4 x 11 1/2", 11" h.
....**$300-350**

Japanese Miniature Bracket Clock with Mother-of-Pearl Inlaid Case

Japan: Miniature mother-of-pearl inlaid rectangular case w/beveled top w/ring handle, sliding front & rear panels, brass dial plate w/floral engraving rotates behind a single vertical hand, calendar indications show in two little openings below the time dial, one showing the 12 terrestrial branches, the other the 10 celestial branches, stepped base w/bracket feet, intricate floral displays on all surfaces, original winding key in hidden drawer, fusee time & strike movement w/verge controlled by a balance rotating under the bell, made before Japan adopted Western timekeeping about 1873, mid-1800s, 6" h. **$11,200**

Junghans Music Box Bracket Clock with Ribbed Quatrefoil Dome

Junghans (Germany): Wooden case w/music box in domed top, quatrefoil flattened dome ribbed top w/brass bail handle, molded pediment over border inset w/beads, two half-round Ionic columns w/gilt bases & capitals flanking dial panel w/arch-topped glass-paned door & corner decoration, molded bottom w/border matching pediment, stepped base on gilt square wafer feet, the silvered metal dial w/black Roman numerals & ornate gilt spandrels & arch decoration, eight-day time & strike movement w/Swiss Thorens disc-playing music box activated by clock movement at the hour, w/comb intact & 18 discs & original disc box, ca. 1920, 21 1/2" h...$3,360

*German Mahogany-Case Bracket Clock with Stepped
Bottom Molded on Flat Tab Feet*

Linden (Germany): Mahogany case w/a domed top & metal loop
handle, the square glass front w/molding over a dial w/Roman
numerals & applied gilded spandrels, stepped bottom molded on
flat tab feet, eight-day time & triple chime movement, ca. 1940s,
7 1/2 x 11", 14 1/2" h. **$350**

Seth Thomas English Design Walnut-Case Bracket Clock

Thomas, Seth: Walnut case w/domed top & brass loop handle, brass & enamel dial w/Roman numerals, based on an 18th c. English design, eight-day time & strike movement w/floating balance, ca. 1950s, 3 3/4 x 7 1/2", 10 1/2" h..............................**$180**

Winterhalder & Hoffmeier Oak-Case Bracket Clock with Ribbed Quatrefoil Dome

Winterhalder & Hoffmeier (Germany): Oak case w/cove molded pediment topped by ringed stemmed orb corner finials & ribbed quatrefoil dome on beveled base, the square brass dial frame w/cast spandrels & center, the steel chapter ring w/black Roman numerals, the case w/reeded side pilasters w/Corinthian capitals, ribbed & beveled decoration at top & bottom, the molded block base w/molded feet, quarter striking time & strike movement, ca. 1900, 15" h. **$616**

*Winterhalder & Hoffmeier
Oak-Case Bracket Clock with
Molded Bracket, Ogee Sides,
and Carved Apron*

Winterhalder & Hoffmeier (Germany): Oak case w/molded pediment w/panel of carved decoration topped by flat-topped dome w/carved decoration, the case w/reeded pilasters w/Corinthian capitals flanking the arched brass dial panel w/heavy cast foliate spandrels & three subsidiary dials in the arch above the main dial, each dial w/steel chapter rings, the time dial w/brass Arabic numerals, the subsidiary dials for tune selection (four or eight gongs), the sides of the case w/inset panels w/intricate carving, the bottom w/a band of carved decoration over the molded block base, chime/silent & F/S regulation, quarter-chiming three-train time & strike movement plays Whittington or Westminster tunes, comes w/original molded bracket w/ogee sides & carved apron, ca. 1890, 22" h., w/bracket 33 1/2" h. **$4,592**

Calendar Clocks

Ansonia Brass and Copper Company Octagonal Short-Drop Calendar Clock with Mahogany-Veneer Case

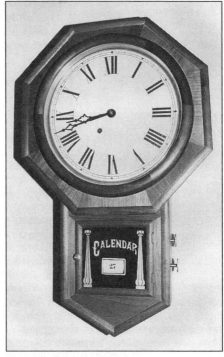

Ansonia Brass and Copper Company: "Novelty Calendar" mahogany-veneered octagon, short-drop simple calendar clock, exact copy case, eight-day, time only, spring driven, 10 1/2" d. dial, 17" w., 26" h.

....**$700** for copy, **$1,000** for original

L.F. & W.W. Carter Double-Dial Calendar Clock with Rosewood-Veneer Case

Carter, L.F. & W.W.: Double-dial calendar, molded rosewood veneer case w/cove molded base drop, the large round top molding around the white painted time dial w/black Roman numerals & subsidiary hand pointing to days of the week, the long drop case enclosing the smaller calendar dial w/Arabic numerals for dates & subsidiary hand pointing to months, both dials w/wooden bezels & original hands, eight-day weight time & strike movement of Welch manufacture, clean label inside case & B.B. Lewis label on back of calendar dial, some flaking to time dial, minor lifting of veneer, small dings in bezels, two iron weights not original, ca. 1865, 31" h. **$1,688**

L.F. & W.W. Carter Weight-Driven Double-Dial Perpetual-Calendar Clock with Rosewood Case

Carter, L.F. & W.W.: Rosewood perpetual-calendar clock w/double dial, ca. 1863-68, eight-day, time only, weight driven, top dial 17 1/2" d., bottom dial 11 1/2" d., 22" w., 59" h. **$2,500**

L.F. & W.W. Carter Double-Dial Perpetual-Calendar Clock with Rosewood Case

Carter, L.F. & W.W: Rosewood double-dial perpetual-calendar, top dial records days & bottom dial records months & dates, eight-day, time & strike, 13 1/2" w., 21" h. **$600**

DuBois and Fils Silver-Case Calendar Clock with Spread-Winged Eagle Finial

DuBois & Fils (Switzerland):
Tall silver case w/round top dial section w/notched rim & topped by spread-winged eagle finial, a white porcelain time dial w/Arabic numerals framed by a/polychrome scene at top showing a man holding dog & looking toward draped columns, two subsidiary dials for date & days of the week, raised on a flattened waisted support w/a bulbous lower body w/applied flower decoration, all supported by two figural satyrs standing on a rectangular stepped base w/bands of notched decoration & leaf & bead trim, key-wind calendar movement, chain fusee movement w/monometallic balance just visible behind the fancy gilt cock that fits in dial, both dial & movement signed, replaced crystal, ca. 1830, 7" h..**$1,960**

French Double-Dial Calendar Clock with Belgian Slate Molded Case

France: Double-dial type, Belgian slate rectangular molded contour case on molded contour block base, both dials in white porcelain w/brass bezels & center rings, the upper time dial w/black Roman numerals, the lower calendar dial w/perpetual indications & moon phase & a central equation of time hand that points to the month & to a ring of numerals that gives the minutes each day that sunlight is increasing or decreasing, time & strike movement w/open escapement, ca. 1875, 16" h. **$2,352**

German Calendar Clock Set with Bell and Clear Cut-Glass Inkwells Topped with Trojan Figures

Germany: "Inkwell Calendar Clock" set, a rectangular stepped black base supporting a central upright round clock w/bell on top & top ring handle, the white dial w/brass bezel, black Roman numerals for time & red Arabic numerals in outside ring for dates, two subsidiary dials, one black & one red hand, clock flanked by two matching square clear cut-glass inkwells w/brass-hinged integral covers in the form of helmeted Trojans, each on its own stepped square base, ca. 1915, 13" w., 9 1/2" h....................**$896**

W.L. Gilbert Short-Drop Calendar Clock with Walnut Case

Gilbert, W.L.: Walnut round top, short-drop simple calendar clock w/G. Maranville's calendar movement, patent 1861, eight-day, time only, spring driven, 14 1/2" d. dial, 17 1/2" w., 33 1/2" h. $1,500

*W.L. Gilbert
"Elberon" Model
Oak-Case
Calendar Clock*

Gilbert, W.L.:
"Elberon" oak
simple calendar
shelf clock
w/McCabe's
November 10,
1896 patent cal-
endar movement,
repainted tablet
has flowers
instead of birds,
this clock was
sold by the
Southern
Calendar Clock Company in the late 1890s, eight-day, time &
strike, spring driven, 8" d. dial, 15" w., 30 1/2" h. **$1,700**

E. Ingraham, & Company "Ionic Calendar" Model Perpetual-Calendar Clock with Rosewood Case and Double Dial

Ingraham, E. & Company: "Ionic Calendar" model, double-dial perpetual-calendar model w/a rosewood figure-eight case, wide round upper molding enclosing the time dial w/Roman numerals & subsidiary dial pointing to days of the week, slightly smaller round lower molding enclosing the B.B. Lewis calendar dial w/Arabic numerals for the days of the month & subsidiary dial pointing to the months, a small roundel on each side of the case center, eight-day time & calendar movement, original label in case back, top bezel w/small dry split, upper dial darkened w/age, cover on back of calendar dial missing, ca. 1888, 29 1/2" h...**$1,680**

Ithaca "Cottage" Model Calendar Clock with Walnut Case and Double Dial

Ithaca: "Cottage" walnut calendar clock w/double dial, H. B. Horton's calendar patents, April 18, 1865, & August 28, 1866, eight-day, time & strike, spring driven, 5" d. upper dial, 7" d. lower dial, 12" w., 25" h. **$1,000**

*Ithaca Ionic
Cast-Iron-Case
Perpetual-
Calendar Clock
with Double Dial*

Ithaca: Cast-iron ionic perpetual-calendar wall clock using H.B. Horton's calendar movement as seen on bottom dial, eight-day, time only, 9" w., 19" h. **$2,500**

*Ithaca "No. 4"
Model Walnut
Perpetual-Calendar
Clock with Double
Dial*

Ithaca: "Number 4"
walnut perpetual
calendar with H.B.
Horton's perpetual
calendar movement
patent 1865, eight-
day, time and strike,
double spring driv-
en, 12" d. upper
dial, 9" d. lower
dial, 31" h. $15,000

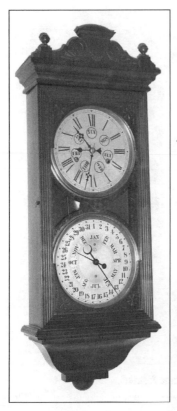

Jerome & Company Hanging-Model Wooden-Case Calendar Clock with Double Dial

Jerome & Company: "REG-ISTER, Hanging" model, wooden case w/molded cornice w/arched crest & corner knob finials, beveled frame around glass pane over the upper time dial w/Roman numerals & subsidiary dial pointing to days of the week, the lower calendar dial w/Arabic numerals for dates & subsidiary dial pointing to months, both dials w/brass bezels, on molded base w/ogee drop & short finial, time & strike movement, some discoloration to time dial, ca. 1880, 31" h. **$1,792**

*Macomb Calendar
Clock Company
Walnut-Case
Perpetual-Calendar
Clock with Double
Dial*

**Macomb Calendar
Clock Company:**
Walnut perpetual-cal-
endar clock, ca.
1882-1883, incised
carving, moon phas-
es on lower dial, eight-day, time & strike,
13" w., 28" h. $4,800

Macomb Calendar Clock Company Walnut-Case Perpetual-Calendar Clock with Double Dial

Macomb Calendar Clock Company: Walnut perpetual-calendar clock w/double dial Seems' calendar & eight phases of the moon, movement by E.N. Welch, ca. 1882-83, eight-day, time & strike, spring driven, 6" d. dial, 14 1/2" w., 30" h...**no price available**

New Haven Double-Dial Perpetual-Calendar Clock

New Haven: Perpetual-calendar shelf clock, w/two parallel dials, inscribed lines, eight-day, time only, 14" w., 13" h. **$2,200**

New Haven
"Cabinet No. 7"
Model Double-Dial
Calendar Clock

New Haven: "Cabinet No. 7" model, ash case w/uncommon dial configuration, the calendar dial forming the top of the case in molded frame w/leaf crest & side garnishes, the calendar dial w/black Arabic numerals & months, the time dial centered in body w/brass bezel & center ring & black Roman numerals, the rectangular body w/contour frame, beading on top & inset w/panels w/various molded or carved decorations, on molded base, time & strike movement, ca. 1885, 21 3/4" h...$2,016

*Prentiss Clock Company
Mahogany-Case Spring-
Driven Calendar Clock*

Prentiss Clock Company:
Mahogany calendar clock, ca.
1890, 60-day, time only, double spring movement &
spring driven calendar that
only needs to be wound once
a year, 9 1/2" d. dial, 12" w.,
36" h. $2,500

Sessions Oak-Case Spring-Driven Calendar Clock

Sessions: Oak calendar clock, early 1900s, eight-day, time only, spring driven, 16 1/2" w., 36" h. **$500**

Southern Calendar Clock Company "Fashion No. 2" Model Mahogany-Case Calendar Clock

Southern Calendar Clock Company: Mahogany "Fashion No. 2," calendar clock, eight-day, time & strike, Pat. July 4, 1876. The cases & the time movements were made by Seth Thomas & the calendar mechanism used was the Andrews Calendar patent. The company was located in St. Louis, Missouri. **$1,500**

Seth Thomas
"No. 5" Model
Walnut-Case
Calendar
Clock with
Double Dial

Thomas, Seth:
"No. 5" walnut
double-dial cal-
endar clock
w/R.T. Andrew's February 15, 1876, patent calendar movement,
eight-day, time & strike, spring driven, 7" d. dials, 12 1/2" w.,
20" h. $950

Seth Thomas "No. 10" Model Walnut-Case Perpetual-Calendar Clock with Double Dial

Thomas, Seth: "No. 10" walnut perpetual-calendar shelf clock w/applied & turned decorations. Provisions for the date, day & month are on the lower round tablet, eight-day, time & strike, weight driven, 36" h. **$4,000**

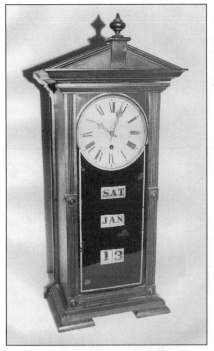

*Waterbury
Walnut-Case
Calendar Clock
with Roller-Type
Calendar
Movement*

Waterbury: Walnut simple calendar shelf clock, ca. 1890, w/roller type calendar movement, eight-day, time only, spring driven, 7" d. dial, 13 1/2" w., 32" h. **$2,500**

*Waterbury
Walnut-Case
Perpetual-
Calendar Clock
with Double Dial*

Waterbury: Walnut, double-dial perpetual-calendar shelf clock, A. F. Well's, July 30, 1889, patent calendar movement, eight-day, time & strike, spring driven, 7" d. dials, 16 1/2" w., 29" h.
....$1,400

Waterbury "Calendar No. 36" Model Oak-Case Calendar Clock with Double Dial

Waterbury: "Calendar No. 36," oak case w/scrolling crest flanked by round ringed corner blocks w/finials & molded pediment, body w/contour design side splats & half-round ropetwist columns w/urn-form capitals & bases, glass-paned front panel over the white dials w/brass bezels, the upper time dial w/brass center ring & black Roman numerals, the calendar dial w/Arabic numerals & rollers, the molded base w/long ornately carved back splat & shallower apron in front w/molded scroll design, time-only movement, original glass & pendulum, old key, some paint flakes, date wheels darkened from age, ca. 1891, 28" h. **$2,352**

*E.N. Welch
Octagonal
Short-Drop
Calendar Clock
with Oak-
Veneer Case*

Welch, E.N.: Oak-veneered octagon, short-drop simple calendar clock, dated 1887, eight-day, time & strike, spring driven, 17" w., 24" h. **$500**

Welch, Spring & Company Rosewood-Case Perpetual-Calendar Clock with Double Dial

Welch, Spring & Company: Rosewood calendar clock w/B.B. Lewis's perpetual movement, patented Dec. 18, 1868, eight-day, time & strike, 11" w., 20" h. $1,050

Welch, Spring & Company Double-Dial Calendar Clock with Wood-Veneer Case

Welch, Spring & Company: Variant of "Round Head Regulator No. 2," wood-veneer case w/molded round top over the time dial & simple molded drop w/calendar dial, time dial w/Roman numerals & subsidiary hand pointing to days of the week, the calendar dial w/Arabic numerals for dates & subsidiary hand pointing to months, molded base drop, two-weight time & strike movement, excellent Lewis calendar label, minor flaking & chips, age crack, ca. 1872, 34" h. **$1,120**

Carriage Clocks

*Ansonia Elliptical Dial (Left) and Enameled "Oriole" Model (Right)
Thirty-Hour Carriage Clocks*

Ansonia: Carriage clocks
(Left) Elliptical dial, 30-hour, time only, 2 1/2" wide,
6" h. **$600**
(Right) "Oriole" enameled in colors, w/brass framework,
30-hour, time & alarm, 6 1/2" h. **$550**

Boston Clock Company Brass-Case Carriage Clock with Tandem-Wind Spring

Boston Clock Company: Carriage clock, patented Dec. 20, 1880, brass case, porcelain dial, tandem-wind spring movement, 30-hour, time only, 4" w., 6 1/2" h. $3,750

French Brass Carriage Clock with Anglaise-Style Clock and Embossed Floral Decoration on Dial

France: Brass Anglaise-style case w/embossed gilded bands around top & bottom, case held together by threaded finials on top & screws through ring-turned feet, beveled glass front & sides, gilt-metal dial mask w/white porcelain time dial w/ornate embossed floral decoration in center & subsidiary alarm dial below w/plain gilt center, both w/molded bezels, eight-day time & alarm silvered lever platform movement, front glass w/minor chip, ca. 1900, 6 1/4" h. **$392**

French Brass-Case Carriage Clock with Low Bracket Feet

France: Brass case w/rounded corners & beveled glass front & sides, top handle, low bracket feet, white porcelain rectangular dial w/black Arabic numerals & subsidiary alarm dial, cylinder platform time-only movement w/alarm, minor chips on glass, ca. 1910, 5 3/4" h. $420

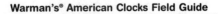

*French Brass-Case
Carriage Clock with
Turned Bun Feet*

France: Brass case
w/top handle,
embossed bands
around top & base molding, turned bun feet, beveled glass front &
sides, the dial w/Roman numerals & subsidiary seconds dial
marked "J.E. Caldwell Co. - Philadelphia," original lever platform,
time only movement w/alarm, replaced minute hand, made in
France, retailed by Caldwell, ca. 1900, 5 3/4" h. **$336**

French Brass-Corniche-Case Carriage Clock with Molded Bracket Base

France: Brass Corniche case w/rounded corners, cornice & molded bracket base, bail handle at top, beveled glass front & sides, white porcelain dial w/black Roman numerals & subsidiary seconds dial, grand sonnerie w/alarm, selector lever on base engraved w/"Gde Sonnerie, Silence, or Hours & Quart's," ca. 1909, 7" h. $1,344

French Brass-Doucine-Case Carriage Clock with Top and Bottom Bands of Embossed and Gilded Rococo Scrolls

France: Brass Doucine case w/serpentine-sided top & bottom bands decorated w/bands of embossed & gilded rococo scrolls, flat scroll-shaped bail handle on top, beveled glass front & sides, gilt-metal dial mask w/white porcelain chapter ring w/black Arabic numerals & original hands, short ringed round wafer feet, eight-day time-only cylinder platform movement, ca. 1900, 6 1/4" h. $336

*French Cast-Brass
Carriage Clock with
Foliate Design*

France: Cast brass
upright rectangular
case w/overall foliate
design & bail handle
at top, beveled glass front & sides, white porcelain dial w/black
Roman numerals & subsidiary dial, time, strike, alarm & repeat
lever platform movement w/butterfly extension on lever, backplate
of movement signed "Bechot & Fils, à Paris" & numbered 133,
bottom cover & one case screw missing, ca. 1850, 6 3/4" h.
....**$1,344**

French Gilded-Brass-Case Carriage Clock with Molded Pediment and Base

France: Gilded-brass-case w/molded pediment & base, bail handle, beveled glass front & sides, the square white dial w/black Roman numerals, subsidiary seconds dial & original hands, backplate signed w/"D-C" trademark w/tiny carriage clock between & serial number 13661, selector lever for "Striking" & "Silent" on base, petit sonnerie w/alarm, ca. 1890, 6 1/4" h...**$1,064**

French Gilded-Brass-Case Carriage Clock with Porcelain Panels of Birds, Butterflies, and Flowers

France: Gilded-brass case w/molded top & cove molding over plain base w/block feet, square corners, angled bail handle at top, glass front & two sides each w/porcelain panels of birds, butterflies & flowers, the white chapter ring w/black Arabic numerals, time & strike movement w/original silvered lever platform intact, "Harris & Shafer, Washington" on dial mask, ca. 1905, 7 1/2" h. $2,576

French Brass-Case Carriage Clock with Stepped Cornice

France: H&H, rectangular brass case w/stepped cornice w/straight ring handle, beveled base & bracket feet, beveled glass front & sides, white dial w/Arabic numerals, original lever platform, time, strike & repeat movement, replaced minute hand, ca. 1900, 5 3/4" h. **$420**

French Miniature Brass-Case Carriage Clock with Cupid on Front Porcelain Panel

France: Miniature upright brass case w/enameled porcelain panels under the beveled glass on front framing the dial & on the sides & top, the inset top panel depicts a pair of doves, the sides show pastoral scenes w/lovers dressed in lavender, pink, blue, red & white, the front shows Cupid w/bow lying under the dial near a tree that branches around dial, simple bail top handle & block base, the white porcelain dial w/brass bezel & star-like center ring & black Roman numerals, time-only movement w/tiny lever platform spanning the top of the plates, tiny chip in glass, hairline in porcelain, ca. 1900, 3 1/2" h. w/handle **$1,680**

French "Pendule D'Officer"-Style Carriage Clock with Gold-Plated Domed Case

France: "Pendule D'Officier"-style, gold-plated domed case w/ornate overall decoration, the top w/a flat rectangular platform for the scrolled bail handle, white porcelain glass-paned dial w/black Roman numerals & hands & signed w/dealer's name, "Lescurieux & Cie.," flattened knob feet, time & strike movement, ca. 1880, 8 1/4" h. **$2,016**

*French Petite
Sonnerie-Type
Brass-Corniche-Case
Carriage Clock*

France: Petite son-
nerie-type, upright
brass Corniche case w/rounded corners, molded top w/scroll
bail top handle, beveled glass on front & sides, dial w/Roman
numerals, on a block base w/bracket feet, time & strike movement w/lever platform strikes ding dong quarters & full hours &
quarters on demand, comes w/original leather traveling case
minus strap, ca. 1900, 7" h. **$1,568**

French Round Ormolu-and Brass-Case Carriage Clock with Scrolling Leaf-Design Handle

France: Round ormolu & brass case w/pierced design around sides, scrolling leaf-design handle & short feet, round glass front over white porcelain dial w/Arabic numerals, platform cylinder escapement mounted on the back plate, movement marked "France," ca. 1900, 5 1/4" h. $252

French Brass "Anglaise Riche" Case Carriage Clock with Fluted Corinthian Columns

France: Upright brass "Anglais Riche" case w/fluted Corinthian columns & fluted top bail handle, dentil borders at top & bottom, beveled glass panels on front, sides & top, striped & spotted dial mask, white porcelain dial w/black Roman numerals, gilt minutes & original hands, signed "G. Edward & Sons, London & Glasgow" for the retailer, block base w/molding at top & square wafer feet, time, strike, repeat & alarm lever platform movement numbered 6172, ca. 1900, 7 3/4" h..................**$1,960**

German Brass-Case Carriage Clock with Brass Lyre-Form Pendulum

Germany: Brass case w/tall beveled glass front & sides framed by colonettes enclosing a steel dial w/Roman numerals suspending a brass lyre-form pendulum, ca. 1950s, 3 1/2 x 6 3/4", 10 1/2" h. **$180-200**

Ch. Hour Grand Sonnerie-Type Gilt-Brass Carriage Clock with Floral Engraving on Sides and Top

Hour, Ch. (France): Grand Sonnerie-type, gilt-brass upright rectangular gorge case w/floral engraving on sides & top, twisted bail top handle, beveled glass panels on front & sides, gray porcelain dial w/black Arabic numerals, original hands & subsidiary dial directly underneath, thin bracket feet, 13-jewel time, strike & alarm movement w/lever platform signed "Ch. Hour, France - 13 - Thirteen Jewels," made for Tiffany & Co., ca. 1900, 7 1/4" h..**$4,200**

*F. Kroeber
Brass-Case
Carriage
Clock with
Glass Sides*

Kroeber, F.: Carriage clock, ca. 1889, brass case, glass sides, time only, 8" h. **$200**

*Chs. Oudin Brass
Carriage Clock with
Rococo Decorations
and Gargoyles on Top
Corners*

**Oudin, Chs.
(France):** Gilt-brass
upright rectangular
case ornately cast
w/Rococo style blos-
soms, swags, scrolls &
leaves, gargoyles at
each top corner, elabo-
rate cut-out scroll bail
top handle, glass front
& side panels, the gilt-
metal dial surround
w/intricate engraving, the white porcelain dial w/black Arabic
numerals & signed "Chs. Oudin - Paris," subsidiary dial directly
underneath, time, strike, scroll & leaf feet, a face in relief w/frame
forming apron at base, repeat & alarm movement numbered
13859 w/single coiled gong struck from above for the hours &
from the underside for the alarm, most of the gilding rubbed off,
ca. 1880, 7 3/4" h. **$2,800**

Wm. Rossiter "#3528" Model Brass-Case Carriage Clock with Acorn Finials

Rossiter, Wm.: (London, England): "#3528" model, gilt-brass upright rectangular case w/molded pediment & base, bail handle on top, round columns at each corner below acorn finials, the sides & front all w/finely engraved decoration, round white porcelain dial w/black Roman numerals & gilt-brass bezel, the rear w/door for winding & setting the hands & engraved silvered plaque w/Rossiter's name & clock's number, circular wafer feet, time-only movement, small hairline in dial, ca. 1825, 4 3/4" h. **$1,904**

Cartel Clocks

French Louis XVI-Style Cartel Clock with Ornate Ribbon, Vine Top, and Leaf and Flower Cornucopia Borders

France: Louis XVI-style, gilt bronze, ornate openwork works, ribbon & vine top suspending the round enameled dial w/Roman & Arabic numerals surrounded by large scrolling leaf & flower cornucopia borders, a twisted ribbon pendent base drop, two train chiming movement, early 20th c., 14" w., 35" h. $3,105

French Cartel Clock with Ovoid Oak Case, Carved Rococo Scrolls, and Finials of Grapes and Grape Leaves

France: Ovoid oak case w/heavily carved rococo design of scrolls w/crest & drop finial of carved grapes & grape leaves, molded circular wooden dial w/black Roman numerals on white porcelain cartouches, original pierced-brass hands, time & strike movement strikes the hours & half hours on coiled wire gong, ca. 1890, 28" h. $532

French Gilt-Bronze Louis XVI-Style Cartel Clock with Lyre-Form Case and Tall Neck Below a Domed Canopy and Scrolls

France (probably): Gilt-bronze Louis XVI-Style case, the lyre-form case flanked by putto terms holding a wreath, the tall neck centered by a sphinx term below a domed canopy & scrolls, the lower case cast also w/delicate floral bands around the round dial w/enameled Roman numerals, ca. 1900, retailed & signed by J.E. Caldwell & Company, Philadelphia, overall 55" h. $2,875

French Victorian Carved Cartel Clock with Baroque-Style Walnut Case and Leaf, Fruit, and Scroll Designs

France: Victorian carved Baroque-style walnut case w/leaf, fruit & scroll designs w/ebony accents, dark round dial w/molded bezel & white number cartouches w/black Roman numerals, replacement movement resulting in three filled holes in backboard, ca. 1890, 27" h. $896

Cottage Clocks

Ansonia Clock Company Cottage Clock with Glass Panel Reverse-Painted with Geometric Gilt Loops

Ansonia Clock Company: Simple dark hardwood case w/veneering removed, upright rectangular case w/a two-pane door, the large upper pane over the large faded dial w/Roman numerals & gilt trim above a narrow rectangular glass panel reverse-painted black w/geometric gilt loops, deep molded base, time & strike, second half 19th c., 4 x 8 1/2", 11 3/4" h..**$90**

J.C. Brown Cottage Clock with Glass Panel Reverse-Painted with Greek-Style Columned Buildings

Brown, J.C.: Upright rectangular rosewood case on slightly stepped block base, two-pane glazed door, the large upper pane over a signed painted dial featuring Roman numerals & painted spandrels of pink flowers & green leaves, the small narrow rectangular lower glass pane reverse-painted w/a scene of Greek-style columned buildings, some in-painting, good label, eight-day signed time & strike movement, some veneer loss, replacement, hands & doorknob, ca. 1855, 15 1/4" h. $560

*Congress
Cottage Clock
with Glass
Panel
Decorated with
Gilt Sprays*

Congress: Walnut cottage shelf clock, ca. 1880, eight-hour, time only, 12" h.. ....$150

Forestville Manufacturing Company Cottage Clock with Glass Panel Reverse-Painted with Large Building Flanked by Roses

Forestville Manufacturing Company: Upright rectangular rosewood case w/beveled frame & base, delicate gold floral decoration on case, the door w/two glass panes, the large upper pane over the dial w/gold floral spandrels & black Roman numerals, the lower reverse-painted pane w/a center scene of a large building w/trees in background flanked by two panels of roses, eight-day time & strike signed movement, legible label, tiny veneer chips, some paint loss on dial, replacement hands, ca. 1849, 15 1/4" h. $560

Forestville Manufacturing Company Cottage Clock with Ripple-Design Base and Glass Panel with Reverse-Painted Scene

Forestville Manufacturing Company: Wooden ripple w/original glass panels in door, one w/reverse-painted decoration, round dial w/Roman numerals, 30-hour time & strike movement, some flaking on tablet, paint loss on dial, ca. 1849, 15" h. **$364**

*Seth Thomas
Cottage Clock
with Decorated
Panel*

Thomas, Seth: Rosewood cottage shelf clock, circa 1920, time and strike, 13" h.. ....$150

Crystal Regulator Clocks

Ansonia "Admiral" Model Crystal Regulator with Polished Mahogany Base and Top

Ansonia: "Admiral" polished mahogany crystal regulator, finished in rich gold, porcelain dial, mercury pendulum, open escapement, beveled glass, eight-day, time & half hour gong strike, 10" w., 18" h. **$4,000**

*Ansonia "Regal"
Model Crystal
Regulator with
Open Escapement*

Ansonia: "Regal" crystal regulator, finished in rich gold, visible (or open) escapement, mercury pendulum, beveled glass, eight-day, half-hour gong strike, 10 1/2" w., 18 1/2" h. **$4,500**

*Ansonia
"Sovereign"
Model Crystal
Regulator with
Polished
Mahogany Base
and Top*

Ansonia: "Sovereign" polished mahogany crystal regulator, mercury pendulum, beveled glass, visible escapement, eight-day, half hour gong strike, 10 1/2" w., 18 1/2" h. **$3,600**

Ansonia Crystal Regulator with Gold-Painted Cast-Spelter Case

Ansonia: Gold-painted cast-spelter case w/a large urn finial, pierced cast scrolls at the top & base corners, beveled glass front, back & sides, large brass bezel enclosing the enameled dial w/Roman numerals, open escapement, faux mercury pendulum, late 19th - early 20th c., 6 1/2 x 7 1/2", 15 1/4" h. **$700-800**

Ansonia "Peer" Model Brass-Case Crystal Regulator

Ansonia: "Peer" model, brass case w/beveled glass front & sides, ornate scroll design on cornice, base, trim & doorknob, trifid feet, round porcelain dial w/brass bezel & black Roman numerals, original fancy pendulum, eight-day time & strike movement, glass chips on door & back panel, ca. 1917, 12" h. **$599**

Boston Clock Company "Alhambra" Model Crystal Regulator with Gold-Plated Case

Boston Clock Company: "Alhambra" crystal regulator, patented Dec. 20, 1880, beveled glass, gold-plated case, 11-jeweled movement, porcelain dial, tandem wind movement, eight-day, time & strike, 14" w., 23 1/2" h. When new, cost was $133; now it is valued at...**$3,750**

Boston Clock Company "Delphus" Model Crystal Regulator with Brass Case

Boston Clock Company: "Delphus" model, upright rectangular brass case w/reeded columnar corners & beveled top w/notched & beaded panels below, beveled glass sides & front, round porcelain dial w/applied gilt numbers, bezel & center decoration, original hands, molded base w/beaded rim on top, bracket feet, nickel-plated rear plates w/"damaskeen" finish, eight-day time & strike 11-jewel lever movement, ca. 1890, 10 1/2" h. **$952**

Davies Mirror-Back (Left) and Wooden-Case (Right) Crystal Regulators

Davies:
(Left) "Crystal Gem" mirror-back shelf clock, patented March 23, 1875, eight-day, time & strike, spring driven, 16" h. **$700**
(Right) Wooden-case shelf clock w/warrior head on pendulum, eight-day, time & strike, spring driven, 16" h. **$700**

French Bow-Front Brass-Case Crystal Regulator

France: Bow-front brass case w/cloisonné corner panels enclosing beveled glass front & sides, top w/brass molding & quatrefoil cloisonné decoration, more cloisonné in top & bottom borders, molded bracket base, gilt dial w/Arabic numerals, original hands & center sunburst pattern, eight-day time & strike movement, made in France for J.E. Caldwell & Co., Philadelphia, ca. 1900, 11 1/4" h..**$1,568**

French Crystal Regulator with Domed Brass Case

France: Domed brass case w/molded arched top & molded base each w/rounded corners & bracket feet, beveled glass in front & sides, white porcelain dial w/brass bezel & center ring, black Roman numerals & open brocot escapement, grid pendulum w/large bob, time & strike movement, minute hand too short, some hairlines in chapter ring, ca. 1900, 18 1/2" h. **$1,960**

*French Crystal
Regulator with
Brass Molded
Frame*

France: Simple
upright brass
molded frame on
bracket feet
w/beveled glass
panels in front &
sides, white
porcelain dial
w/brass bezel & center ring, open escapement & black Roman
numerals, ship's wheel under dial rotates back & forth as long as
the clock is wound, eight-day time & strike movement, some hairlines to dial, ca. 1900, 11 1/2" h......................................**$2,968**

French Crystal Regulator Topped with Crystal Urn

France: Upright case w/quatrefoil flattened arch mahogany top w/large ormolu & cut crystal urn at center, gilt-metal pine cone finial at each corner, four cut & polished crystal columns w/ormolu capitals at corners flanking the glass sides & the porcelain dial ring w/Roman numerals around an engine-turned center w/original gilding, mahogany platform base w/ormolu front ribbon decoration on flattened urn feet, brass mounts, mercury pendulum, rack time & strike movement, signed "Made in France," early 20th c., 15 1/2" h..................................**$3,024**

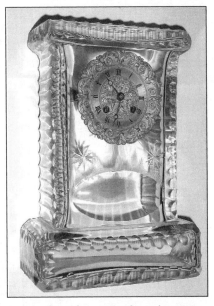

French Crystal Regulator with All-Glass Clear Crystal Cut Case

France: Upright rectangular all-glass clear crystal cut case w/fluted frame & starburst designs on front, block base w/bands of circular decoration, enclosing an ormolu dial & bezel w/ornate scroll, floral & leaf design around chapter ring & in center, black Roman numerals & original moon hands, time & bell strike movement w/silk thread suspension & Mougin trademark, replacement pendulum, ca. 1840, 10" h. $1,036

Gold-Painted Crystal Regulator with Cast-Spelter Case

Gold-Painted Cast-Spelter Upright Case: w/an arched top w/five flower basket finials, an egg-&-dart cornice over a scroll-cast panel above the long beveled glass door & sides, porcelain dial w/Arabic numerals & decorated w/flower swags, glass tube pendulum, rectangular platform base cast w/a scroll & floret band on flat tab feet, eight-day time & strike movement, early 20th c., 5 3/4 x 8 3/8", 15" h. $600-650

Seth Thomas "Empire No. 10" Model Crystal Regulator

Thomas, Seth: "Empire Number 10" crystal regulator shelf clock, ca. 1900, eight-day, time & strike, spring driven, 8" wide, 6 1/2" deep, 14 1/2" h. **$700**

Seth Thomas "Empire No. 65" Model Crystal Regulator with Brass Bow-Front Case

Thomas, Seth: "Empire No. 65" model, brass bow-front case w/slightly arched stepped cornice, four fluted columns at sides & aproned base w/block feet, white dial w/Arabic numerals & bezel, columns missing some gold finish, ca. 1909, 11" h. **$504**

Vermont Clock Company Crystal Regulator with Brass Case

Vermont Clock Company: Upright rectangular brass case w/rounded corners & beveled top, beveled glass panels in front & sides, round white porcelain dial w/brass bezel, black Roman numerals & original hands, two-jar mercury pendulum, molded base w/bracket feet, damascened nickel-plated round eight-day time & strike movement w/time train located outside main plates, ca. 1915, 9 1/2" h. $672

Waterbury Crystal Regulator with Polished Brass Case

Waterbury: Polished brass crystal regulator, mercury type pendulum, open escapement, time & strike, 7" w., 9 1/2" h.
....**No price available**

Cuckoo Clocks

American Cuckoo Clock Company Neo-Gothic Arts & Crafts Cuckoo Clock

American Cuckoo Clock Company: Fumed oak Neo-Gothic Arts & Crafts case, stepped flat top above Gothic arched & flat pilasters flanking the cuckoo door & brass dial w/Arabic numerals, eight-day weight-driven movement, time & strike, oak pendulum bob in a wheel design, tall obelisk-shaped iron weights, early 20th c., 5 1/4 x 9 1/4", 12 3/4" h. plus chain & weights (illustrated disassembled) $200-250

German Cuckoo Clock with Oak Leaves and Carved Pheasant on Walnut Case

Germany: Wood case w/walnut peaked roof carved w/oak leaves cascading along the top & down the sides centered by a carved pheasant perched on peak, the round dial w/darker wood chapter ring, carved hands & white Roman numerals, the arched base covered w/carved ferns & forest plants, a steer standing below the dial, heavy brass 56-hour time & strike movement, old bird, nice tone on old flutes, bellows recovered, ca. 1925, 24" h. **$1,680**

German Cuckoo Clock with Vines and Spread-Winged Bird on Wooden Case

Germany:
Wooden house-shaped case w/pairs of leaves on vines twining up from base to peaked "roof," spread-winged bird finial, beveled base w/valanced skirt & bracket feet, original dial w/bone hands & grommets around winding holes, Roman numerals, cuckoo w/articulated beak & wings, original flutes, time & strike movement, cast lyre-shaped plates geared for 56 hours, ca. 1920, 15" h. **$980**

German Cuckoo Clock with Carved Wooden Chalet-Style Case

Germany: Carved wood chalet-style case, 30-hour movement, ca. 1950, 9" w. **$225**

Keebler Time-Only Cuckoo Clock with Bird Atop Molded-Wood Case

Keebler: "Coo-Coo" clock in original box, never used, molded wood, 30-hour, time only, 4 1/2" w., 7" h.. ....**$150**

Keebler Time-Only Pendulette Cuckoo Clock with Red and Green Foliage on Molded-Wood Case

Keebler: Cuckoo pendulette, molded wood, red & green foliage, 30-hour, time only, spring driven, 5" w., 6 1/2" h.. ....$125

*Keebler
Time-Only
Pendulette
Cuckoo
Clock with
Green Leaves
on Molded-
Wood Case*

Keebler: Cuckoo pendulette, molded wood, green colored leaves, 30-hour, time only, spring driven, 3 1/2" w., 6" h.. ....**$55**

Keebler Time-Only Pendulette Cuckoo Clock on Molded-Wood Case

Keebler: Cuckoo pendulette, molded wood, 30-hour, time only, spring driven, 4" w., 5" h. **$45**

Keebler Time-Only Pendulette Cuckoo Clock with Colored Foliage and Bluebird on Molded-Wood Case

Keebler: Cuckoo pendulette, molded wood, green leaves & red flowers, bluebird feeds its babies, 30-hour, time only, spring driven, 4" w., 5" h.. ....**$45**

Keebler Time-Only Pendulette Cuckoo Clock with Spread-Winged Eagle on Molded-Wood Case

Keebler: Pendulette, molded wood, spread winged eagle at the top, green leaves, 30-hour, time only, spring driven, 4" w., 5" h. ..
....**$45**

Lux Time-Only Pendulette Cuckoo Clock with Molded-Wood Case

Lux: Cuckoo pendulette, molded wood, bird sitting on top, 30-hour, time only, spring driven, 4" w., 6" h.. ....$45

Lux Time-Only Pendulette Cuckoo Clock with Original Box

Lux: Cuckoo pendulette w/original box marked, "Lux Pendulette Clock—a Novelty Clock by Lux," 30-hour, time only, spring driven, 4" w., 7" h. **$150**

Lux Time-Only Pendulette Cuckoo Clock with Bird Atop Molded-Wood Case

Lux: Cuckoo pendulette, molded wood, bird sitting at the top, 30-hour, time only, spring driven, 4 1/2" w., 7" h. **$55**

Lux Time-Only Pendulette Cuckoo Clock with Bird Atop Molded-Wood Case

Lux: Cuckoo pendulette, molded wood, bird sitting at the top, 30-hour, time only, spring driven, 8 1/2" w., 11 1/2" h. **$200**

Lux Time-Only Pendulette Cuckoo Clock with Green Leaves and Bluebird on Molded-Wood Case

Lux: Cuckoo pendulette, molded wood, green leaves & bluebird, time only, spring drive, 4" w., 5" h. $45

Lux Time-Only Pendulette Cuckoo Clock with Bird Atop Molded-Wood Case

Lux: Cuckoo pendulette, molded wood, bird sitting on the top, 30-hour, time only, spring driven, 4" w., 6 1/2" h. **$45**

*Time-Only
Pendulette
Cuckoo Clock
with
Multicolored
Wood Case*

Unknown maker:
Multi-colored
wooden pend-
ulette cuckoo
clock, 30-hour,
time only, spring-
driven. $65

Gallery Clocks

Hammond Clock Company Metal-Case Electric Gallery Clock

Hammond Clock Company: Metal case Postal Telegraph "Synchronous Electric Time" gallery wall clock, ca. 1931, 15" d. dial. **$75**

E. Ingraham Spring-Driven Gallery Clock

Ingraham, E.: Gallery clock, ca. 1900, time only, spring driven, 16" d. **$900**

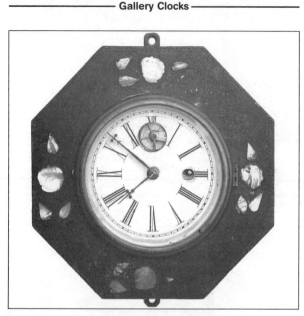

N. Pomeroy Iron-Case Octagonal Gallery Clock

Pomeroy, N.: Iron octagonal case painted black w/mother-of-pearl inlaid accents around the sides framing the round white dial w/black Roman numerals, open escapement & brass bezel, hangers at top & bottom cast into iron backboard, 30-hour lever/balance time-only movement signed "N. Pomeroy," loss of paint on case, ca. 1850, 9" h. **$392**

Samuel Emerson Root Metal-Case Gallery Clock

Root, Samuel Emerson: Metal wall clock w/case made by Nicholas Muller, ca. 1850, eight-day, time only, marine movement, 5" d. dial, 12" outside d. ....**No price available**

A..D. Smith Civil War Commemorative Gallery Clock

Smith, A.D.: Marine movement gallery-style clock made to commemorate Civil War, S.B. Jerome patented round case, a flat simulated leather over pine round frame w/brass trim featuring pressed-brass stars, bugles & crossed swords bordered in brass, the central round dial w/Roman numerals, missing seconds hand, Hubbel eight-day time-only movement, original label, ca. 1868, 13" d. $728

Seth Thomas "One Day Lever" Model Gallery Clock with Rosewood-Veneer Molded Case

Thomas, Seth: "One Day Lever" model, gallery-type, 10-sided rosewood veneer molded case, a large brass bezel enclosing glass over the painted dial w/subsidiary seconds dial ring & black Roman numerals, good label on back, 30-hour time & strike lever movement, some paint loss on dial, ca. 1880, 13" h. **$308**

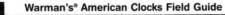

Seth Thomas Walnut-Case Gallery Clock

Thomas, Seth: Walnut gallery clock, 15-day, time only, 18" d. dial, 25 1/2" outside d.. ....$2,500

Seth Thomas Spring-Driven Metal Case Gallery Clock

Thomas, Seth: Metal-case gallery clock, 30-day, time only, spring driven, 13" d. dial, 22" outside d. **\$900**

Seth Thomas Oak-Case Gallery Clock

Thomas, Seth: Oak gallery clock, 30-day, time only, 17" d. dial, 20" outside d. **$900**

Seth Thomas Oak-Case Gallery Clock

Thomas, Seth: Oak gallery wall clock, ca. 1890, 30-day, time only, 24" d. **$600**

Waterbury Spring-Driven Oak-Case Gallery Clock

Waterbury: Oak gallery clock, 30-day, time only, spring driven, 23" d. dial, 30" outside d. **$2,000**

Glass-Dome Clocks

Ansonia "Crystal Palace No. 1" Glass-Dome Clock with Two Figures

Ansonia: "Crystal Palace Number 1" w/two figures under glass dome, mercury pendulum, time & strike, 15" w., 19" h.
....**$1,800**

George W. Brown "Briggs Rotary" Model Glass-Dome Clock with Wooden-Footed Round Base and Metal-Ball Pendulum

Brown, George W.: "Briggs Rotary" model, wooden footed round base & glass dome enclosing the metal-framed dial w/Roman numerals w/the metal ball pendulum suspended at the front, early production model w/John C. Briggs, patents of Aug. 1855 & July 1856 stamped on top plate, early spider cast-metal winding key on bottom, original Roman numeral dial, bezel & pendulum bob, hands are old replacements, time & strike movement, ca. 1860, 7 3/4" h. $672

Coe & Company Glass-Dome Clock with Papier-Mâché Case Decorated with Gilt Scroll and Mother-of-Pearl Floral Designs

Coe & Company: Papier-mâché, the scrolled front embellished w/gilt, polychrome & mother-of-pearl floral designs, housing the circular enamel dial inscribed "Saml. S. Spencer" & lever spring-driven movement, all mounted on a decorated oval base on brass ball feet under glass dome, labeled "Botsford's Improved Patent Timepiece manufactured by Coe & Co. 52 Dey Street, New York," 11" h. **$1,265**

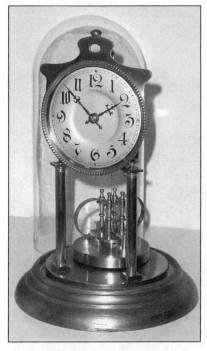

Jahresuhrenfabrik Art Nouveau Glass-Dome Clock with Stepped Round Base

Jahresuhrenfabrik (Germany): Art Nouveau style 400-day clock, upright brass frame w/the dial raised on brass columns set on a stepped round base, large round silvered metal dial w/raised chapter ring, beaded brass bezel, contour splat & black Arabic numerals, compensating pendulum, produced for Carp Year-Long Clock Co., adjusting shaft on pendulum broken in center, early gimbal suspension, replacement glass dome, ca. 1902, 11" h. **$571**

Japanese Annular Glass-Globe Clock with a Small Fish Forming the Pendulum and a Bigger Fish Revolving Around the Dial

Japan: Annular clock set in a clear glass globe enclosing the orbital dial on shaft w/two animated fish keeping time, a smaller fish forms pendulum & wiggles back & forth w/each tick, the bigger fish does a full revolution around dial one tick at a time, globe set on beveled chrome base w/Art Deco geometric decoration, six molded saucer feet, time-only movement, ca. 1950, 5" h.
....**$1,176**

*Chauncey Jerome
Glass-Dome Clock
on Oval Base with
Brass Feet*

Jerome, Chauncey:
Brass-front footed
timepiece w/ornate
scrolling design on
oval base w/brass
feet & h.p. decora-
tion, glass dome
cover, white dial w/Roman numerals, Botsford Patent 30-hour
movement w/mono-metallic balance, some cracks to dial & dome,
base decoration worn, ca. 1850, 11" h..................................$616

Kienzle Glass-Dome Clock with Circular Brass Stepped Base and Brass Disc Pendulum

Kienzle (Germany): 400-day clock, brass framework w/scalloped crest w/three small finials all supported on brass columns w/turned capitals & bases, a brass bezel enclosing the round white dial w/black Arabic numerals, brass disc pendulum, all on circular brass stepped base, gimbal suspension, unit serial number 20825 on both rear plate & pendulum, old glass dome, ca. 1905, 11" h...$448

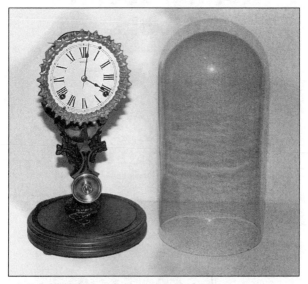

E. N. Welch Skeleton-Style Glass-Dome Clock

Welch, E.N.: Skeleton shelf clock, w/glass dome, late 1800s, eight-day, time & strike, spring driven, 9 1/2" d., 16" h.
....**No price available**

Gothic/Beehive Clocks

Birge & Mallory Beehive Clock with Mahogany Case

Birge & Mallory: Mahogany beehive shelf clock w/a J. Ives patented movement, ca. 1838-43, eight-day, time & strike, wagon-spring driven, 14" w., 26 1/2" h.. ....**$2,500**

*Brewster &
Ingraham
Beehive Clock
with Mahogany
Molded Case*

**Brewster &
Ingraham:**
Beehive mahogany
molded case on
rectangular base,
round molding
over the glass
door over dial
w/Roman numer-
als, rectangular
glass door
beneath w/cut
glass tablet, eight-
day time & strike
rack & snail
movement, Kirk's
Patent iron backplate, fading & paint loss to dial, lower panel
probably a replacement, ca. 1844, 19" h. **$1,008**

*Brewster &
Ingraham
Beehive Clock
with Burled
Walnut Case*

Brewster & Ingraham: Burled walnut beehive shelf clock, brass springs, replaced tablet & hands, eight-day, time & strike, 10 1/2" w., 19" h. **$400**

*Brewster &
Ingraham
Beehive Clock
with
Mahogany
Ribbed Case*

Brewster & Ingraham: Mahogany ribbed beehive shelf clock, original brass springs replaced, eight-day, time & strike, 10 1/2" w., 19" h. **$450**

*J.C. Brown
Beehive Clock
with Rosewood
Case*

Brown, J.C.:
Rosewood bee-
hive shelf clock,
ca. 1855, dial
reads: "J.C.
Brown,
Forestville
Company,"
replaced tablet,
eight-day, time & strike, 10 1/2" w., 19" h..........................**$400**

*J.C. Brown
Beehive Clock
with Rosewood
Ribbed Case*

Brown, J.C.: Rosewood ribbed front Beehive shelf clock, ca. 1855, time & strike, 10 1/2" w., 19" h.. ....**$1,200**

*Seth Thomas
Beehive Clock
with Walnut
Case and
Westminster
Chimes*

Thomas, Seth: Beehive style, the upright peaked walnut case w/a glass door opening to a steel dial w/Arabic numerals & small speed & chime adjustment dials all backed by ornately scroll-incised gilt brass, molded base, eight-day movement w/Westminster chimes, ca. 1920, 7 3/4 x 10 1/2", 14 3/4" h.
....**$600-700**

Seth Thomas Beehive Clock with Mahogany Case and Westminster Chimes

Thomas, Seth: Mahogany beehive shelf clock, eight-day, time & Westminster chimes, spring driven, 10" w., 15" h.................**$690**

Seth Thomas "Prospect No. 1" Model Beehive Clock with Mahogany Case

Thomas, Seth: "Prospect No. 1" mahogany beehive shelf clock, ca. 1910, time & strike, 13 1/2" h. **$220**

Tiffany Battery-Operated Beehive Clock with Mahogany Case

Tiffany: Battery operated mahogany beehive shelf clock, ca. 1895, beveled glass, time only, 10" w., 16" h............................**$1,250**

Victorian Gothic-Revival-Style with Carved Mahogany Three-Spire Case

Victorian Gothic Revival Style:
Carved mahogany, the case carved in the form of a Gothic arch w/three spires enclosing a glazed arch door over the engraved silver dial w/Roman numerals & a small seconds dial, blocked base, French two-train half-strike movement, retailed by Shreve, Crump & Low, late 19th c., 19 1/2" h.......................**$805**

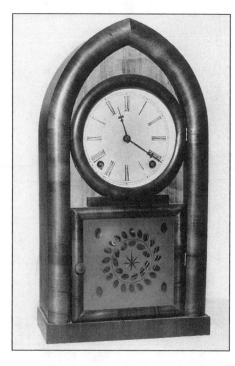

E.N. Welch
"Beehive"
Model Beehive
Clock with
Rosewood
Case

Welch, E.N.: "Beehive Model" rosewood shelf clock, eight-day, time & strike, spring driven, 6" d. dial, 10 1/2" w., 19" h.............**$350**

*E.N. Welch
Beehive Clock
with Rosewood
Case*

Welch, E.N.: Rosewood beehive shelf clock, all original, ca. 1860 to 1870, 10 1/2" w., 19" h. **$350**

Grandfather Clocks

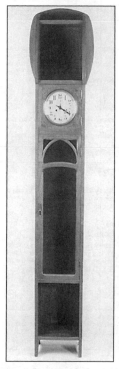

Arts & Crafts-Style Grandfather Clock with Oak Case and Oblong Top Backboard

Arts & Crafts Style: Tall slender oak case w/an oblong top backboard behind an open compartment over a square door w/scroll-carved corners flanking the round bezel opening to a round dial w/Arabic numerals above a tall slender amber glass door w/arched loop at the top, an open compartment at the bottom, low arched bootjack feet, applied brasses, Europe, early 20th c., 86 1/4" h..**$1,265**

Blunt & Company Gothic-Revival-Style Grandfather Clock with Mahogany and Mahogany-Veneer Case and Three Spires

Blunt & Company: Gothic Revival style, mahogany & mahogany veneer, the hood w/molded Gothic arched cornice w/central plinth & spire flanked by smaller spires above a round molded brass bezel enclosing a round engraved silver regulator dial w/Arabic numerals & signed by the maker, the waist w/a tall glazed Gothic arch door framed by crossbanding above a crossbanded rectangular panel flanked by lambrequin corners over the tall base section w/slender cut-out feet, eight-day weight-driven movement, old finish, ca. 1840, minor imperfections, 94 1/2" h. $12,650

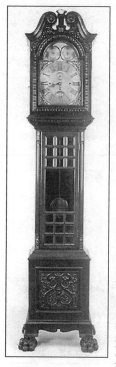

Colonial Revival Grandfather Clock with Carved Mahogany Case, Broken-Scroll Pediment, and Lotus-Form Finial

Colonial Revival: Carved mahogany case, broken-scroll pediment centered by a lotus-form finial & carved w/rosettes & scrolling decoration above the arched glazed door bordered by carved beading, beveled glass door opening to an arched gilt-brass & silvered metal dial w/two small upper dials over the main dial w/Roman numerals & ornate spandrels, the upper case flaring out & bead-carved above the long case fitted w/a long door w/nine small square beveled panes above & below the large beveled central pane showing the large brass pendulum, the stepped-out lower case w/an ornately scroll-carved central panel over a scalloped apron & boldly carved hairy paw feet, Westminster & Whittington chimes, retailed by Bigelow, Kennard & Co., Boston, late 19th - early 20th c., overall 95" h. $4,888

*Colonial Revival "Elite" Model
Grandfather Clock with Oak Case
and Carved Urn Finials*

Colonial Revival: "Elite" model, dark carved oak case, a high broken-scroll front pediment w/a large central carved urn finial & smaller corner urn finials w/smaller broken-scroll pediments & finials at the sides of the top, an arched glazed top door over the arched dial w/moon phase movement over the brass filigree-trimmed dial w/brass Arabic numerals, the tall waist w/rows of small raised square panels at each side & a glazed tall front door opening to the large weights & flanked by quarter-round columns at the sides, the stepped-out bombé base section w/a lappet-carved band above wide bands of scroll carving, on carved paw feet, nine-tube three-weight movement, late 19th - early 20th c. **$14,850**

Walter Durfee Colonial Revival Grandfather Clock with Walnut Case, High Broken-Scroll Pediment, and Pineapple Finial

Durfee, Walter: Colonial Revival-style walnut case, a high broken-scroll pediment centering a large carved pineapple finial above the swag- & ribbon-carved frieze band above the arched glazed door opening to a steel dial w/brass Arabic numerals below the moon phase dial all flanked by free-standing colonettes & cloth-lined lattice-work sides on a projecting cornice over the waist section topped by a band of leafy swag carving above an arched, geometrically-glazed front door flanked by columns & w/glazed sides, the projecting base section w/shaped panels centering swagged leaf & blossom carving, carved base band above scroll-carved feet, tube striking movement, retailed by Tiffany & Co., New York, late 19th - early 20th c., 102" h. **$20,000**

Elliot Gothic-Revival Grandfather Clock with Mahogany Case, Gothic Arch Crest, and Westminster and Whittington Chimes

Elliott (London, England): Gothic Revival mahogany case, the Gothic arch crest topped by a large flame-style finial & flanked by spiked spire corner finials over the arched glass door opening to a moon phase dial over the clock dial w/Arabic numerals, the lower glass panel of the door w/Gothic arch muntin opening to the weights & chimes, the door flanked by blocked pilasters above the paneled base platform w/Gothic trefoil carving, molded base band on beveled bun feet, dial labeled "Elliott, London," brass works w/tubular Westminster & Whittington chimes, w/key & pendulum w/its mercury vials removed, England, late 19th - early 20th c., 97" h. $7,700

Elliot Renaissance-Style Grandfather Clock with Pair of Winged Griffins Atop Carved-Oak Case

Elliott (London, England):
Renaissance-Style carved oak case, the arched pediment mounted w/a pair of winged griffins flanking a central shield above a panel of acanthus leaf carving over another arched panel of leaf carving above the ornate filigree dial w/Arabic numerals & a moon phase action flanked by columns over a scroll-carved band above the tall waist w/a paneled door finely carved w/delicate fruit & flower vines flanked by reeded columns, the stepped-out base w/a gadrooned band around the top above leafy scroll & shield-carved panels above the flared stepped base on paw feet, two-train quarter striking movement on gongs, ca. 1890, 104" h..$13,800

English Queen Anne-Revival Grandfather Clock with Arched Top and Ball and Spike Finials

England: Queen Anne Revival mahogany case w/arched top & brass corner ball & spike finials, molded cornice above ogee side splats & simple colonettes w/brass capitals & bases flanking the arched glazed door opening to the 12" brass dial w/black Roman numerals framed by cast shell spandrels & a sunburst in arch, tall center case w/a long wood door, deep molding atop the stepped-out base w/a molded panel on the front, serpentine apron & bracket feet, eight-day signed Salisbury movement striking on a giant cathedral gong mounted to the back of the case, door key in bag taped to movement, small dry splits & scrapes, knob to top door has been pulled out & screwed into nearby location, ca. 1900, 86" h. **$1,736**

French Grand-Sonnerie Grandfather Clock with French-Provincial Oak Case and Large Brass Bob

France: Grand sonnerie-type, French Provincial oak case w/rectangular top w/molded pediment, a narrow floral-carved frieze band on front, a narrow carved molding around the tall front glass pane over the round white dial w/brass bezel & black Roman numerals & the bar pendulum w/large brass bob, tall lower case section w/a rectangular carved molding enclosing carved fruit cluster, molded base w/carved edges raised on circular wafer feet, three-train Morbier time & strike movement strikes two bell quarters followed by full hours on a third large bell, brass-sheathed weights, spider web crack in dial, black dial mask not original, minor dings in bob, replacement weights, ca. 1860, 97" h. **$3,920**

*French Gothic-Revival Grandfather
Clock with Oak Case and Ornate
Gothic Arch with Five Spires*

France: Oak Gothic Revival style tall
case, the ornate Gothic arch-carved
top enclosing the signed round steel
dial w/Arabic numerals above the tall
narrow case w/a two-panel Gothic
arch & linenfold-carved narrow door
flanked by quarter-round ropetwist
edge bands, the stepped out base section w/a carved linenfold panel above
the flared rectangular foot, late 19th
c., 12 x 22", 95" h..$8,050

Frank Herschede Clock Company Gothic-Revival Grandfather Clock with Mahogany and Mahogany-Veneer Case and Pointed Arch Crest

Herschede, Frank, Clock Company: Gothic Revival style mahogany & mahogany veneer case, pointed arch crest w/wide molding above a tall arch-topped door w/the upper section covering the steel dial w/Arabic numerals below a moon phase movement, the lower door w/Gothic arch glazing opening to the large weights & large pendulum, long pilasters down the sides of the case, octagonal block front feet, early 20th c. $3,650

Frank Herschede Clock Company "Model 215" Grandfather Clock with Mahogany Case, Arched Top, and Whittington and Westminster Chimes

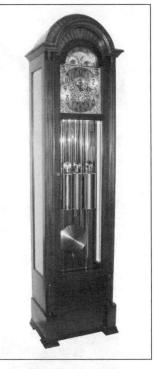

Herschede, Frank, Clock Company: "Model 215," mahogany molded case w/arched top & stepped base, beveled glass panels in front & sides, the ornate brass dial plate & steel chapter ring w/black Arabic numerals below the arched rolling moon phase section, slender reeded columns down the front above the deep, slightly stepped-out base section on flat block feet, nine-tube two-tune (Whittington & Westminster) time & strike movement, door lock intact & w/original Herschede-signed winding crank, minor repair to top dust cover, ca. 1950, 80" h. $2,464

William Herwick Federal-Style Grandfather Clock with Inlaid Mahogany Case and Broken-Scroll Pediment

Herwick, William: Federal-style inlaid mahogany case, the molded broken-scroll pediment above an arched frieze band w/line inlay over the set-back arched door opening to a painted dial w/Roman numerals & a moon phase dial & flanked by slender colonettes, the tall waist w/decorative band inlay flanking the tall door w/corner fan inlay & a central oval inlaid band, the stepped-out lower case w/further decorative inlay banding & an inlaid central circle, on small French feet, signed indistinctly, untouched & unrestored, early 19th c. $8,750

*Ithaca Spring-Driven
Grandfather Clock with Oak
Case*

Ithaca: Oak grandfather clock,
ca. 1920, eight-day, time &
strike, spring driven, 11 x 18",
82" h. **$750**

Renaissance-Revival-Style Grandfather Clock with Figures Flanking Carved Walnut Case

Renaissance Revival Style: Carved walnut, a male & a female caryatid flanking either side of hood, the face w/painted lunar phases in arch, brass mounts & subsidiary dials, the case w/glass door flanked by carved terms, square base w/winged beast terms to sides, carved paw feet, late 19th c., 97 1/2" h...............................**$9,775**

Rich & Holt Grandfather Clock with American-Made Oak Case, English-Made Movement, and Cast-Iron Bell

Rich & Holt: Oak grandfather clock (case made in America), ca. 1920, 30-hour, strikes hour on cast-iron bell (English made movement), 19" w. at top, 82" h. $1,750

Benjamin Rittenhouse Chippendale Grandfather Clock with Cherrywood Case, Broken Swan's Neck Pediment, Pinwheel Terminals, and Urn and Flame Finials

Rittenhouse, Benjamin: Chippendale carved cherrywood, the broken swan's neck pediment w/pinwheel terminals & urn & flame finials above an arched glazed door opening to an engraved brass dial inscribed "BENJAMIN RITTENHOUSE - FECIT 1790," w/second hand, date hand & moon phase dial flanked by colonettes, the arched door below flanked by fluted quarter-columns above a "turtle-mounted" base w/similar columns on ogee bracket feet, ca. 1780, 11 x 19 1/4", 99" h. **$17,250**

Seth Thomas "Grandfather Look" Floor Clock with Upper Clock Resting on Lower Storage Section

Thomas, Seth: Mahogany custom-made "grandfather look" floor clock, w/OG upper section resting on top of lower storage section, 30-hour, 19" wide, 77 1/2" h.
....$700

Waltham Clock Company Kit-Built Grandfather Clock with Mahogany Case

Waltham Clock Company:

Mahogany grandfather clock, made from a kit, early 1900s, brass weights & pendulum, beveled glass, applied brass decorations, moon dial, 91" h. $1,500

Waterbury Weight-Driven Time-Only Jeweler's Regulator Floor Clock with Oak Case

Waterbury: Oak jeweler's regulator floor clock, eight-day, time only, weight driven, 13 x 31", 105 1/2" h. **$8,000**

Luman Watson Federal-Style Grandfather Clock with Cherry Case, Mahogany Accents, Broken-Scroll Pediment, and Urn Finials

Watson, Luman: Federal style cherry case w/mahogany accents, broken-scroll pediment w/urn finial & matching corner finials, slender baluster-form colonettes flanking the arch-top glass door over the signed dial w/delicate floral spandrels & black Arabic numerals, the simple tall case w/narrow wooden door flanked by beveled front corners, base section w/top molding & inset panels on front & sides, cove molding at bottom above short baluster-turned feet, 30-hour Hoadley-type wooden time & strike movement, dial w/small chip & minor loss of black, door glass w/small crack, winding barrel w/small chip on rim, ca. 1820, 94" h. **$4,704**

*Whitehurst Renaissance-Style
Grandfather Clock with Oak Case,
Broken-Scroll Crest, and Three
Brass-Ball Finials*

Whitehurst (Derby, England):
Renaissance-Style oak case, a broken-scroll crest w/three brass-ball
finials over the scroll-carved frieze &
arched glazed door flanked by elongated scroll carvings & opening to
the metal dial w/Roman numerals &
a moon phase & date crest above the
narrow case w/narrow front panel
carved w/scrolls above a full-length
carved figure of a standing medieval
king over a grotesque mask panel,
all flanked by slender carved Gothic-
style side caryatids, the lower case
w/a scroll-carved panel flanked by
carved mask & scroll corner bands
over the deep scroll-carved apron,
two-train chiming movement, late
19th c., 9 5/8 x 18 1/4",
92 1/2" h. **$2,645**

Lantern Clocks

English Brass-Case Lantern Clock with Domed Top, Ring-Turned Finial, Overhanging Dial, and Knob Feet

England: Upright brass case w/a bell forming the domed top w/ring-turned finial, four straps attach finial to matching corner finials, the front w/a circular dial w/Roman numerals overhangs the case, the center w/engraved leafy scroll decoration, reticulated floral panels between the straps over the domed top & on four sides between corner finials, sides of case w/engraved decoration, corner ring-turned columns ending in knob feet, eight-day chain fusee time & strike movement strikes the hour on the top bell, chapter ring has lost its silver, movement a bit gummy, ca. 1890, 15 1/4" h....................**$1,232**

Thomas Wheeler Lantern Clock with Brass Case, Overhanging Dial, Silvered Chapter Ring, and Bun Feet

Wheeler, Thomas (London, England): Brass case, the sides w/hinged plates, the top bell w/straps applied to finials centering pierced plates, the silvered chapter ring w/Roman numerals centering an alarm indicator, w/one hand, on bun feet, signed "Thomas Wheeler near ye French Church, London," Charles II period, late 17th c. **$4,889**

Mantel-Garniture Clocks

French Mantel-Garniture Set with Pair of Candelabra and Crystal Regulator

France: Clock & pair of candelabra, ormolu & bronze crystal regulator clock w/stepped pediment topped by a figural spread-winged eagle, the case w/glass sides & ormolu columns on either side of arched glass dial panel below ormolu winged horse mounts on a dark green bronze panel, the white dial w/ormolu bezel & center & black Roman numerals, the pendulum decorated w/concentric rings of tiny leaves, a narrow dark green bronze panel w/further ormolu mounts below the dial door, on a molded rectangular ormolu base w/stepped feet, time & strike movement w/Marti Medaille D'Or trademark; the candelabra each w/four candleholders, the center one inset w/a flame finial, each w/curlicue embellishments raised on green bronze shafts w/ormolu ringed capitals & bases, on square bases similar to clock's w/ormolu decorations on front bronze panel, ca. 1900, 22" h., the set $2,464

French Mantel-Garniture Set with Pair of Urns and "Amour et Psyché" Model Figural Clock On Marble Bases

France: Clock & two urns; "Amour et Psyché" model, spelter w/pantinated bronze finish, large cast figures of Cupid & Psyche embracing on a domed mound enclosing the small white dial w/brass bezel & black Arabic numerals, all resting on an ovoid base w/rim of cream & light pink marble w/gray veining & tiny brass ringed feet, eight-day pendulum time & strike movement; the matching urns w/scrolling outcurved side handles & long necks topped w/domed covers & flame finials, on stepped ring-turned outcurved shafts on marble bases similar to clock's, ca. 1900, 22" h., the set..**$1,960**

French Mantel-Garniture Set with Art Deco Urns and Crystal Regulator Clock

France (for Wm. Batty & Son, Manchester): Clock & pair of urns; Art Deco style, all pieces of gilded metal w/fine engraving filled w/multicolor enamel floral decoration, the crystal regulator clock case of rounded rectangular form w/radiused sides, top & bottom, on short legs w/ball feet & molded scroll & shell decoration, glass front & sides, topped by scroll-handled covered urn similar to the two matching covered six-sided urns w/straight slender side handles sharply angled at top & square bases w/beveled corners & ring-turned feet (urns convert to candlestands by inverting covers), the gilt dial w/Roman numerals & open escapement, the dial center & surround & pendulum bob also w/colorful enamel decoration, time & strike movement, ca. 1910, 19 1/2" h., the set **$2,800**

*Japy Mantel-Garniture Set with Pair of Urns and "Le Raison" Model
Figural Clock on Green- and White-Veined Marble Bases*

Japy (France): Figural clock set w/matching urns, "Le Raisin"
("The Grape") model, bronze patinated white metal figures &
clock case & urns, each on a green & white veined rectangular
beveled marble base w/gilt flower-form feet, the center piece w/fig-
ure of barefoot woman in clinging garment sitting w/ewer in one
hand & the other arm reaching up to a cherub that stands above
the clock case holding a/basket of grapes, a brass bezel around
the round white porcelain dial w/black Arabic numerals, the short
clock pedestal base w/a brass plaque inscribed "LE RAISIN," gilt-
metal scroll decoration on front of marble base, the urns w/taper-
ing lids w/upturned rims & trifid finials, ornate C-scroll side handles, molded decoration w/grape motif throughout, round French
time & bell strike movement signed, ca. 1900, 14 1/2" h.....**$728**

Junghans Mantel-Garniture Set with Green Onyx Swinging-Arm Clock and Pair of Facing Statues

Junghans (Germany): Swing clock & two facing statues;, gilt cast-metal clock case w/ornate decoration on top & bottom of round white dial w/black Arabic numerals, decorated swing arm w/spiked ringed orb bob, the top of the arm connected to green onyx column w/stepped circular base & gilt-metal accents, side statues of bronze patinated metal, titled "L'Epav" & "Le Sauveteur" after originals by Moreau, one features a woman in diaphanous gown & flowing hair shielding her eyes w/one hand, the other features a scantily clad male holding a rope, both figures on molded domed stepped base on green onyx socles w/title plaques on front, time-only movement, ca. 1900, 11 1/2" h., the set............**$1,568**

Metal-Front/Metal-Case Clocks

American Clock Company Gothic-Style Iron-Front Clock with Bronze Finish

American Clock Company: Gothic-style iron-front case w/bronze finish, the Gothic-arch facade cast w/flowering vines, round brass bezel around the white dial w/Roman numerals above a center panel of repainted red, white & green flowers over a small round pendulum window, block-molded base, 30-hour movement, time only, ca. 1855, 12" h. $280

American Clock Company Multi-colored Metal-Case Clock with Birds and Flowers

American Clock Company: Metal-case shelf clock, multi-colored w/birds & flowers on case, 30-hour, time & strike, spring driven, 13" w., 16" h.. ....$400

Ansonia Spring-Driven Iron-Front Clock

Ansonia: Iron-front shelf clock, ca. 1880, eight-day, time only, spring driven, 10 1/2" w., 12 1/2" h. $300

Ansonia Metal-Front Clock with Gilded Case and Porcelain Dial

Ansonia: Metal-front mantel clock, gilded case, porcelain dial, eight-day, time & strike, 7 1/2" w., 10 1/2" h. **$250**

Ansonia Metal-Case Clock with Syrian Bronze Finish and Porcelain Dial

Ansonia: Metal mantel clock w/Syrian bronze finish, porcelain dial, open escapement, eight-day, time & strike, 11" w., 17 1/2" h. **$600**

*Bradley & Hubbard Rectangular Iron-Case Clock with
Gold-Painted Decoration and Spandrels*

Bradley & Hubbard: Rectangular iron case w/rounded corners
on heavy beveled base, gold-painted decoration & spandrels,
round dial w/black Roman numerals, replaced brass bezel, B&H
label inside case, 30-hour time & strike movement, some paint
loss, touched-up numerals, ca. 1865, 10 3/4" h....................**$140**

F. Kroeber Brass-Washed Metal-Case Clock

Kroeber, F.: Brass-washed shelf clock, patented May 28, 1878, 30-hour, time & alarm, 5" w., 7" h. **$200**

Lux Spring-Driven Metal-Case Clock

Lux: Metal shelf clock, 30-hour, time only, spring driven, 4 1/2" w., 5 1/2" h. **$45**

New Haven Copper-Washed Metal-Case Clock with Porcelain Dial

New Haven: Copper-washed metal shelf clock w/porcelain dial, eight-day, time only, spring driven, 5" w., 8" h. **$100**

*New Haven
Iron-Case
Clock with
Brass Finish*

New Haven: Iron-case shelf clock w/brass finish, 30-hour, time only, spring driven, 3" w., 6" h. **$95**

New Haven Metal-Front Clock with Cupid Figure

New Haven: Metal-front shelf clock w/cupid figure, 4 1/2" w.,
7" h. **$130**

Parker Clock Company Gilded Cast-Iron-Case Clocks

Parker Clock Company: Metal-front mantel clocks, cupids carrying clocks, gilded cast-iron cases, 30-hour, time only.

(Left) 6 1/2" h. $450
(Right) 5 1/2" h. $400

A.L. Swift Metal-Case Stove-Top Clock

Swift, A.L.: Metal stove-top clock, 30-hour, time only, spring driven, 8" w., 10" h..**$125**

Seth Thomas Nickel-Plate-Over-Brass Metal-Front Clock

Thomas, Seth: Metal-front mantel clock, nickel-plated over brass, minute hand, time & alarm, 7" w., 9" h. **$150**

*Seth Thomas
Gilt-White Metal
Case Embossed
with Art Noveau
Decorations*

Thomas, Seth: Gilt-white metal case heavily embossed w/Art Nouveau floral & whiplash decoration, the head of a woman w/long flowing hair forming the base, white dial w/Arabic numerals & ribbed bezel, eight-day time & strike movement w/gong sounding on the hour & bell on the half hour, gold paint not original, ca. 1905, 12 1/2" h. **$392**

Unmarked Metal-Front Clock with Brass Finish

Unmarked Metal-Front Mantel Clock: Patented Feb. 6, 1904, brass finish, time only, 7 1/2" w., 11" h..............................**$135**

Unmarked Metal-Front Clock with Gilded Case and Porcelain and Brass Dial

Unmarked Metal-Front Mantel Clock: Porcelain & brass dial, gilded case, 30-hour, time only, 3" w., 4" h. **$1,325**

*E.N. Welch Brass-Washed-Case Clock with Open Escapement (Left)
and E.N. Welch Brass-Washed-Case Clock with Lever Movement
(Right)*

Welch, E.N.:
(Left) Brass-washed shelf clock w/open escapement, 30-hour,
time only, spring driven, 5" w., 7" h. **$200**
(Right) Brass-washed shelf clock w/lever movement, 30-hour,
time only, 6-1/2" w., 8" h. **$200**

*Westclox
"Ironclad"
Model Alarm
Clock with
Iron Case on
Molded Base*

Westclox: "Ironclad" model alarm clock, rectangular cast-iron case w/rounded corners on molded base, spandrels around white round dial w/black Arabic numerals & notched brass bezel, one-day time-only movement, alarm-set hand on rear missing, ca. 1935, 5 1/4" h **$88**

Western Clock Manufacturing Company Brass-Finished Iron-Front Clock with Female Figure

Western Clock Manufacturing Company: Brass-finished iron-front shelf clock w/female figure holding up the clock, 30-hour, time only, 6 1/2" w., 12" h. **$175**

Mirror Clocks

*Austin Chittenden
Rosewood-Case Mirror
Clock with Wooden Works*

Chittenden, Austin: Rosewood, mirror shelf clock, wooden works, ca. 1831-37, 30-hour, time, strike, & alarm, weight driven, 16" w., 41" h. **$1,000**

Hopkins & Alfred Clock Company Mirror Clock with Mahogany Case and Wooden Works

Hopkins & Alfred Clock Company: Mahogany mirror shelf clock, ca. 1825, wooden works, weight driven, time & strike, 17" w., 30 1/2" h. $425

*Elisha
Hotchkiss
Mirror Clock
with Mahogany
Case and
Wooden Dial
and Movement*

**Hotchkiss,
Elisha:**
Mahogany mirror shelf clock,
dated 1835, 30-hour, time & strike, weight driven w/wooden dial & movement, top repainted but all original. **\$350**

Chauncey Jerome Mirror Clock with Rosewood-Veneer OG Mirror Case

Jerome, Chauncey : Rosewood-veneer OG mirror wall clock, 30-hour, time & strike, ca. 1848, 15" w., 25 1/2" h.. ....**$250**

*Mitchell,
Atkins &
Company
Mirror Clock
with
Mahogany-
Veneer Case*

**Mitchell,
Atkins &
Company:**
Mahogany-
veneered mir-
ror shelf clock w/artificially grained columns & gold stenciling
above dial, ca. 1830-36, 30-hour, time, strike, & alarm, weight
driven, 16 1/2" w., 32" h.. ....**$500**

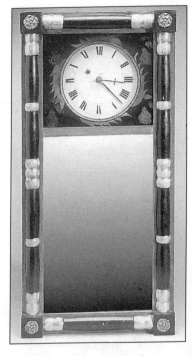

*Benjamin Morrill
Classical-Style
Rectangular-Frame-
Case with Mirror in
Lower Door*

**Morrill, Benjamin
(attributed to):**
Classical style, the rectangular frame case w/a hinged split-baluster border in gilt & black w/the stenciled dial tablet framing the white-painted dial w/Roman numerals, a rectangular mirror in the lower door, w/a brass "wheelbarrow" weight-driven movement, minor imperfections, ca. 1830, 4 x 14", 30" h. **$5,175**

Charles Stratton Mirror Clock with Mahogany-Veneer Case and Gold-Painted Spandrels

Stratton, Charles: Tall upright mahogany-veneer rectangular case, the tall two-pane door w/the upper pane over the dial w/Roman numerals & gold-painted spandrels, long lower pane fitted w/a mirror, superb label, three-train internal alarm time & strike movement w/small weight, professionally refinished case, label dated 1836, 34 1/2" h. **$336**

Eli Terry Mirror Clock with Rosewood Case, Carved Columns, Eagle Splat, and Wooden Works

Terry, Eli:
Rosewood mirror shelf clock w/carved columns & eagle splat, wooden works, ca. 1827, 30-hour, time & strike, weight driven, 20" w., 37" h. **$1,000**

Eli Terry Classical-Style Mirror Clock with Mahogany-Veneer Stenciled Case

Terry, Eli: Classical-style mahogany veneer stenciled case, the flat scalloped pediment stenciled w/a fruit-filled compote & leaves flanked by corner blocks above half-round columns flanking the tall two-pane door, the top glazed pane over a wooden painted dial w/Arabic numerals & gilt spandrels, the lower pane w/a mirror, flat base w/stenciled corner blocks, ivory keyhole escutcheon, eight-day movement, time & strike, ca. 1845, 5 3/8 x 16 1/2", 35" h. **$900-1,000**

Samuel Terry Mirror Clock with Mahogany-Veneer Case and Ivory Escutcheon

Terry, Samuel: Mahogany-veneered mirror shelf clock, w/artificially grained columns & ivory escutcheon, ca. 1829, 30-hour, time & strike, weight driven, 17" w., 34" h. **$400**

*M. Welton
Mirror Clock
with Mahogany
OG Case*

Welton, M.: Mahogany, mirror door OG shelf clock, ca. 1845, repainted dia, 30-hour, time & strike, 16" w., 26" h. **$300**

Novelty Clocks

Ansonia Cast-Iron Black Enamel Novelty Clock with Rotating Ship's Wheel

Ansonia: Cast-iron black enamel novelty mantel clock, with a ship's brass wheel rotating as the escapement moves, seen in 1894 catalog, 15" w., 18 3/4" h...$2,200

Ansonia Jumper Novelty Clocks with Bouncing Figures

Ansonia:

(Left) "Jumper #1" 30-hour, time only, 4" dial, 15 1/2" h.
....**$1,800**

(Right) "Jumper #2" 30-hour, time only, 4" dial, 14 1/2"h.
....**$1,750**

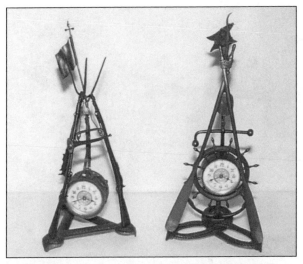

Ansonia Novelty Clocks: Army Rifle-Support Model (Left) and Navy Oar-Support Model (Right), Each with Antique-Brass Finish

Ansonia: Metal novelty clocks with jeweled settings
(Left) "Army" with rifle supports, antique brass, gilt center, porcelain dial, one-day, time only, 2" dial, 12" h..................**$900**
(Right) "Navy" with oar supports, antique brass, gilt center, porcelain dial, one-day, time only, 2" dial, 12" h..................**$850**

Ansonia "Design #2" (Left) and "Design #4" 9 (Right) Early Digital Novelty Clocks

Ansonia:
(Left) Plato "Design #2" early digital novelty clock, patented 1903, time only, 6 1/2" h. **$650**
(Right) "Design #4" early digital novelty clock, patented 1903, time only, 6 1/2" h. **$650**

Austrian Picture-Frame-Style Novelty Clock with Ornate Molded Scrolling Border and Animated Figure of Woodcutter

Austria: Picture-frame style, rectangular gilt plaster frame case w/ornate molded scrolling border, inset cartouche panel w/blue ground surrounded by gilt floral & scroll-decorated mat, gilt bezel, spandrels & flourishes beneath dial w/white chapter ring w/black Arabic numerals, center of dial w/animated figure of Tirolean woodcutter, silk thread time & strike movement strikes the hours & halves on a coiled wire gong & the wood cutter swings his axe at the same time, once for each strike, ca. 1820, 20" h. $2,240

Barnes Smith & Company (Left), J. Becker & Son (Center), and King Alfred Cigar (Right) Novelty Clocks with Cigar Cutters

Barnes Smith & Company:
(Left) Cigar cutter with attached unknown maker clock that is marked "Yale & Co. Jewelers" on dial, 30-hour, time only, spring driven, 14" h. **$1,500**

J. Becker & Son:
(Center) "Bonny Jean" cigar cutter with clock movement ..**$500**

King Alfred Cigar:
(Right) Cigar cutter with attached Waterbury clock, 30-hour, time only, spring driven, 13" h. **$1,500**

French Alarm-Type Novelty Clock with Toulouse-Lautrec Figure That Lights Match

France: Alarm-type, Toulouse-Lautrec, hand moves down when alarm goes off to light a match on clock base & returns to the candle on top, 5 1/2 x 10".........................**$800**

French "Bras en L'Air" Model Novelty Clock with Figure of Gowned Woman with Outstretched Arms That Point to Time

France: "Bras en L'Air" model, the figure of a gowned woman standing w/arms outstretched within an ormolu arch w/swirl columns & shell & spike decorations around top, the woman points to two flanking enamel chapter sectors, one w/hours & one w/minutes, her arms falling when they reach the top, the blue enamel background w/ormolu scroll design throughout, stepped rectangular dark variegated green marble base w/ormolu trim & low square stepped feet, rectangular plated movement w/platform escapement, base w/front-to-back glue repair, feet glued on, crack through numeral 10, ca. 1890, 17" h. **$15,120**

Haddon Clock Company Electric Motion "Home Sweet Home" Model Novelty Clock with Old Woman Rocking and Fire Shimmering

Haddon Clock Company: Electric motion clock, "Home Sweet Home," model of a house in plastic & composition, a square large window over the dial on the left, a window on the right w/a scene of an old woman in a rocker, when plugged in woman rocks & fire shimmers, 20th c., 3 1/2 x 12 1/4", 7 3/8" h. **$185**

French "Magician" Model Novelty Clock with Figure in Turban Lifting Gold Cups on Table

France:
"Magician" automaton, ormolu & bronze, top w/automated Blackamoor figure in formal dress & turban standing at table draped w/star-decorated fringed cloth & lifting inverted gold cups alternately w/his left & right arms & turning his head to right & left, ormolu case w/porcelain dial w/Roman numerals & ormolu hands & signed "Grout, R'de la Feronnerie S.," case front ornately decorated w/floral swags, scrolls & shells scrolling up around dial & extending beyond the case to form cut-out designs at sides & forming apron & heavy outcurved feet, time & strike silk thread movement, ca. 1835, 14 1/2" h..**$28,000**

French "Oarsman" Model Novelty Clock with Paddling Oarsman in Brass Sailboat

France: "Oarsman" model from the Industrial Series, figure of oarsman & clock dial in wrought brass sailboat w/mast & rigging, rudder & tie down, the boat on separate casting of waves mounted to a stepped rectangular red marble base on four gilded skids, the original dial w/Arabic numerals & signed by the London retailer "Dibdin & Co., Ltd, 189 Sloane St, SW-1," eight-day movement, oarsman suspended from a three-point mystery suspension as used in a swinging arm clock & w/a heavy counterbalance that swings down into the base, his paddling motion continuing for full duration of the clock (eight days), ca. 1880, 16 1/2" h. **$12,320**

French "Ship's Quarter Deck" Model Novelty Clock with Moving Helmsman

France: "Ship's Quarter Deck" automata from the Industrial Series, bronze & silvered metal case in the form of a ship's quarter deck, a sailor at the helm on the upper deck gallery w/the clock dial directly below him & flanked by another sailor on one side & the ladder leading to the upper deck on the other, all on a stepped black marble base on gilt brass feet, the gilt dial w/Roman numerals, two-train signed French time & strike movement w/platform escapement & striking the hours & halves on a coiled gong, the helmsman at top forms the top of the compound pendulum & rocks back & forth w/each tick, ca. 1890, 12 1/2" h. **$7,952**

Howard Clock Company Electric "God Bless America" Model Novelty Clock

Howard Clock Company: Electric "God Bless America" wooden shelf clock, patented 1940, 8 1/2" w., 8" h.............................$225

F. Kroeber "Angel Swing" Model Novelty Clock with Figure Swinging Beneath Dial

Kroeber, F.: Pot metal and walnut "Angel Swing" novelty parlor clock, circa 1876, reconditioned case, eight-day, time only, 19 1/2" h...**$2,600**

*Mastercrafter
Electric Motion
Novelty Clock with
Trees Flanking a
Shimmering
Waterfall Scene*

Mastercrafter: Electric motion clock, the tall copper-colored plastic case w/molded green & brown fir trees flanking an opening w/a painted waterfall scene that shimmers when plugged in, ca. 1950s, 5 x 7 1/4", 10 3/4" h. **$125**

Mastercrafters Novelty Clock with Swinging Boy and Girl Figures

Mastercrafters: Plastic case novelty clock with boy and girl swinging as time ticks, time only..$175

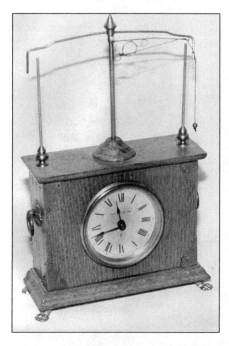

New Haven "Ignatz" or "Flying Pendulum" Model Novelty Clock with Pendulum That Winds and Unwinds Around Side Posts

New Haven manufactured (using the Jerome & Company name): "Ignatz" or flying pendulum shelf clock, with A. C. Clausen Oct. 9, 1883, patent movement, 30-hour, time only, hair spring driven, 7" w., 10 1/2" h. $550

*Oswald
Uhrenfabrik
"Owl" Model
Novelty Clock
with Eyes that
Rotate*

Oswald Uhrenfabrik (Germany): "Owl" model, carved wood model of an owl perched on a wooden base in the form of a book, large eyes rotate when wound, time-only movement, minor nicks & scrapes, ca. 1935, 7 1/2" h...**$644**

Pallwebber Novelty Clock with Digital Pendulum

Pallwebber: Pallwebber's digital pendulum patent is used in this walnut novelty shelf clock. Two windows display the hours and minutes, while a hand shows seconds. Beveled glass, eight-day, time only, 12" wide, 13" h. **$1,000**

Swiss Souvenir "Rue de la Paix" Model Novelty Clock with Street-Lamp Shaped Frame Displaying Rectangular Sign with Street Name

Switzerland: Souvenir, LeCoultre, "Rue de la Paix" model, brass case in the form of a street lamp, the white "lamp" within a brass frame w/ringed finial above the round signed dial w/Roman numerals & pierced hands, all on a ringed shaft tapering out to a circular base, rectangular sign on shaft reads "Rue de la Paix," seven-jewel eight-day movement, ca. 1955, 11" h. $364

*Timby Novelty Clock
with Rotating World
Globe and Walnut
Case*

Timby: Solar walnut
novelty shelf clock
with a world globe
that rotates to indi-
cate the hours, base
dial rotates to register
the minutes, time
only, only 600 of
these clocks were made, 14" w., 27" h. ....**$5,000-$6,000**

Unknown Maker Novelty Clock with Rotating Ferris Wheel From Paris 1900 Exposition

Unknown maker: Metal Ferris wheel novelty clock, souvenir of the Paris 1900 Exposition (printed on tablet), as the clock runs, the Ferris wheel turns, time only, 5" w., 11 1/2" h. **$1,000**

Waterbury Novelty Clock with Rising and Falling
Hand on Elongated Dial

Waterbury: Walnut-stained shelf clock with a hand that goes up
and down and rotates at the top and bottom to show time on this
elongated dial, eight-day, time only, 13" w., 15" h
....**$500-$600**

Octagon Clocks

Ansonia Clock Company "Drop Octagon Extra Cal" Model Short-Drop Octagon Clock with Oak Case

Ansonia Clock Company: "Drop Octagon Extra Cal" model, oak case, octagon top section embossed w/scroll & floral decoration enclosing the round dial w/black Roman numerals for time & smaller Arabic numerals for date, brass bezel & center ring, original hands, the short pointed drop case molded & embossed w/geometric border around a shaped glass pane w/gilt design around oval pendulum window on black ground, eight-day time & strike movement, dial darkened from age & wear, case refinished, glass pane restored to proper design, ca. 1901, 24 1/2" h. $308

Ansonia Clock Company "Office Regulator" Model Long-Drop Octagon Clock with Black-Walnut Molded Case

Ansonia Clock Company: "Office Regulator" model, black-walnut molded case w/octagon top over long drop, white dial w/Roman numerals & subsidiary seconds dial, glass door w/"Regulator" decal in bottom through which pendulum shows, eight-day time & strike movement, new decal, some replacement/restoration, ca. 1901, 32" h. $588

Ball Watch Company Short-Drop Octagon Clock with Oak Case

Ball Watch Company: Oak octagon, short-drop wall clock, ca. 1880, eight-day, time only, spring driven, 12" dial, 24" h.
....$400

L. Hubbell Octagon Clock with Thick Rosewood Case and Patent Lever Escapement

Hubbell, L.: Thick octagon rosewood case w/rounded front, original glazed dial w/brass bezel, black Roman numerals, subsidiary seconds dial & marked "Patent Lever Escapement," signed 30-hour time-only movement, ca. 1870, 6" h. **$252**

*Chauncey Jerome
Short-Drop Octagon
Clock with Mahogany-
and Mahogany-Veneer
Case*

Jerome, Chauncey: Mahogany & mahogany veneer, the octagon-top case w/wide veneer border surrounding a round glazed door over the large dial w/Roman numerals, a short rectangular drop compartment w/angled lower edge & centered by a small decorated glass panel over the short pendulum, ca. 1850,
5 x 17", 22" h. **$2,520**

Sessions Clock Company Short-Drop Octagon Clock with Oak Case

Sessions Clock Company: Octagon short-drop model, golden oak case, the octagonal top w/a large brass bezel over the dial w/Roman numerals, the drop case w/a pointed base & small glazed pointed door w/gilt banding, original finish, replaced eight-day time-only movement, ca. 1900, 5 1/4 x 17", 28" h. **$300-400**

Seth Thomas Octagon Wall Clock with Walnut Case and Brass-Applied Decorations

Thomas, Seth: Walnut octagon wall clock w/brass applied decorations, ca. 1890, time only, 16" w., 25" h. $375

Waterbury Clock Company "Drop Octagon 10 Inch" Model Short-Drop Octagon Clock with Mahogany-Veneer Case

Waterbury Clock Company: "Drop Octagon 10 Inch" model, large mahogany-veneer octagon top enclosing a large brass bezel over the original dial w/Roman numerals & original hands, short pointed drop case w/a small window w/gilt stenciled rings showing pendulum & brass bob, label inside case, eight-day signed time & strike movement, ca. 1895, 21 1/2" h. **$392**

E.N. Welch Manufacturing Company Long-Drop Octagon Clock with Oak Case and Outer Calendar Date Band

Welch, E.N., Manufacturing Company: Octagonal long-drop model, oak case, the octagonal upper section w/a stamped star band around the brass bezel over the dial w/Roman numerals & an outer calendar date band & sweep seconds hand, the pointed drop base w/matching glass door w/stamped star band trim, large stamped brass pendulum bob, original finish, eight-day movement, time only, ca. 1880, 4 x 17 1/2", 33" h. $400-500

OG (Ogee) Clocks

Brewster & Ingraham Double-OG Clock with Rosewood-Veneer Case

Brewster & Ingraham: Rosewood-veneer double-OG wall clock, ca. 1840, 30-hour, time only, 15" w., 25 1/2" h. **$300**

*J.C. Brown
Double-OG
Clock with
Rosewood Case*

Brown J.C.: Rosewood double OG, ca. 1855, original tablet, eight-day, time & strike, 16 1/2" w., 29" h.............................**$350**

*J.C. Brown
Oversized OG
Clock with
Rosewood Case*

Brown J.C.: Rosewood oversized OG, ca. 1855, eight-day, time, strike, & alarm, 16 1/2" w., 31" h...**$350**

*Forestville
Manufacturing
Company OG
Clock with
Mahogany Case*

Forestville Manufacturing Company: Mahogany OG, ca. 1855, w/maker J. C. Brown on the label, eight-day, time & strike, weight driven, 16" w., 29" h..$350

Forestville Manufacturing Company OG Clock with Mahogany Case

Forestville Manufacturing Company: Mahogany OG, ca. 1848, made by J.C. Brown, ca. 1848, eight-day time & strike, weight driven, 17" w., 29" h...$550

*W.L. Gilbert
OG Clock
with
Mahogany
Case*

Gilbert, W.L.: Mahogany OG, eight-day, time & strike, weight driven, 15 1/2" w., 26" h. **$250**

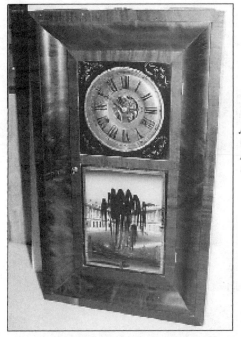

Chauncey Jerome OG Clock with Mahogany Case

Jerome, Chauncey: Jerome invented the case & movement of OG clocks. Shown here is one of his mahogany OG clocks w/brass dial, ca. 1845, 30-hour, time & strike, 15 1/2" w., 26" h...**$300**

Chauncey Jerome Miniature Round-Band OG Clock with Mahogany Case

Jerome, Chauncey: Mahogany miniature round-band OG, ca. 1868, eight-day, time, strike & alarm, tablet not original, 11" w., 16 1/2" h. **$350**

Elisha Manross Double-OG Clock with Mahogany Case

Manross, Elisha: Mahogany double OG, ca. 1845, 30-hour, time & strike, 15 1/2" w., 26" h. $300

*Elisha
Manross OG
Clock with
Mahogany
Case*

Manross, Elisha: Mahogany OG shelf clock, 30-hour, time &
strike, ca. 1848, 15 1/2" w., 43" h. **$300**

Manross Prichard & Company OG Clock and Mahogany Case

Manross Prichard & Company: Mahogany OG shelf clock, ca. 1850, 16" w., 26 1/2" h..**$350**

New Haven Clock Company Miniature OG-Style Clock with Rosewood Case

New Haven Clock Company: Miniature upright OG-style rosewood rectangular case, the tall glass door stenciled w/floral & geometric decoration below the round dial, the white dial w/brass bezel & center ring & black Roman numerals, miniature two-weight time & strike movement, some loss to rear label, ca. 1870, 21 1/2" h. $728

Daniel Pratt Jr. OG Clock with Mahogany-Veneer Case

Pratt, Daniel Jr.: Upright rectangular mahogany- veneer OG case w/two-paned door, smaller upper pane over the dial w/delicate painted spandrels, black Roman numerals & open escapement, the lower pane of frosted glass w/floral & leaf garland engraving, good label w/image of Pratt's Boston showroom, 30-hour time/strike/alarm movement, replacement frosted tablet, some veneer chips, ca. 1850, 26" h. **$196**

Seth Thomas OG Clock with Mahogany Case

Thomas, Seth: Mahogany OG, eight-day, time & strike, weight driven, 15" w., 25" h..**$275**

Seth Thomas Miniature OG Clock with Rosewood Case

Thomas, Seth: Miniature OG rosewood shelf clock, after 1865, 30-hour, time & strike, spring driven, 10 1/2" w., 16 1/2" h. **\$275**

Seth Thomas Miniature OG Clocks with Mahogany Cases

Thomas, Seth:
(Left) Miniature OG mahogany shelf clock, after 1865, eight-day, time & strike, 10 1/2" w., 16 1/2" h. **$175**
(Right) Miniature OG mahogany-veneered shelf clock w/S & T on hands for Seth Thomas, after 1865, 30-hour, time & strike, 10" w., 16" h. **$225**

E.N. Welch Miniature OG Clock with Mahogany Case

Welch, E.N.: Mahogany miniature OG, 30-hour, time & strike, original dial & tablet, 12" w., 19" h. $225

Parlor Clocks

American Clock Company "Parlor" Model Parlor Clock with Walnut Case

American Clock Company: "Parlor" walnut shelf clock, eight-day, time & strike, spring driven, 5" dial, 15" w., 24 1/2" h.
....**$900**

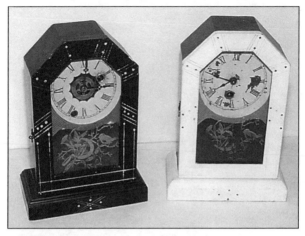

Ansonia 30-Hour Time-and-Alarm Parlor Clocks

Ansonia:
(Left) Black case shelf clock, 30-hour, alarm, 7 1/2" w.,
10 1/2" h. **$100**
(Right) White shelf clock, 30-hour, time & alarm, 7 1/2" w.,
10 1/2" h. **$110**

*Ansonia "Harwich"
Model Parlor Clock
with Cherry Case,
Open Escapement,
and Ceramic Dial*

Ansonia: "Harwich" cherry shelf clock, ca. 1895, open escapement, ceramic dial, time & strike, 12" h..............................**$225**

*Ansonia Gothic
Parlor Clock with
Rosewood Case
and Offset
Pendulum*

Ansonia: Rosewood Gothic shelf clock, ca. 1878, offset pendulum, time only, 10" h. **$135**

*Ansonia Parlor Clock with Walnut-Stained Case,
Hand-Painted Leather Panels, and Open-Escapement*

Ansonia: Walnut-stained case w/hand painted leather panels,
open escapement, eight-day, time & strike, 16" w., 17 1/2" h.
....**$550**

Ansonia "Parisian" Model Parlor Clock with Walnut Molded Case and Arched Top

Ansonia: "Parisian" model, upright walnut molded case w/arched top featuring knobbed finials on crest & turned drop finials at the corners, an arched molded frame enclosing a long glass panel over the brass bezel around the dial w/Roman numerals surrounded by small Arabic calendar numbers, the lower pane decorated w/ornate silver stenciled flower & scrolling vine decoration, the lower sides flanked by S-form brackets, on a deep rectangular stepped base, fancy Ansonia Indicator pendulum, eight-day time & strike movement w/calendar, ca. 1880, 23 1/2" h. **$448**

Ansonia Victorian Renaissance Revival-Style Parlor Clock with Walnut Case

Ansonia: Victorian walnut Renaissance Revival-style case w/a high scroll-carved crest centered by a classical head over the arched, molded cornice w/urn-form finials above an arched glass door w/gilt stencil decoration of cupids & ferns, white dial w/Roman numerals, the door flanked by tall narrow angled mirrors backing gilt-metal standing cupid figures, base w/curved, molded sides flanking a front panel w/gilt-metal scroll boss, eight-day movement, time & strike, third-quarter 19th c., 5 1/2 x 16 1/2", 24 1/4" h...**$750-800**

Benedict Manufactuing Company Parlor Clock with Mahogany Case

Benedict Manufacturing Company: Mahogany shelf clock, medallion below dial, time only, 3 1/2" w., 4" h.. ....**$75**

Wm. L. Gilbert Clock Company "Acheron" Model Parlor Clock with Walnut Case and Stenciled Door

Gilbert, Wm. L., Clock Company: "Acheron" model, walnut case w/fan-carved crest & line-incised scrolls above the arched molded glazed door opening to a dial w/Roman numerals, the lower door w/original silver stenciled leaves, flowers & a checkerboard design, deep flared platform base, paper label inside, late 19th c., 4 1/2 x 13", 19 1/4" h.....................................**$200-250**

Wm. L. Gilbert Clock Company "Lake No. 5" Model Parlor Clock with Walnut Case and Stenciled Door

Gilbert, Wm. L., Clock Company: "Lake No. 5" model, walnut case w/a high ornate scroll-cut & line-incised crest centered by a roundel above a slender half-round turned rail over the tall rectangular glazed door w/a beaded edging, the glass stenciled in silver w/leafy vines & birds, the large dial w/Roman numerals, the brass pendulum decorated w/grape leaves, the lower case trimmed w/further cut scrolls on the deep flaring platform base, eight-day movement, time & strike, ca. 1890, 4 3/4 x 14", 22" h. **$200-250**

Wm. L. Gilbert Clock Company "Lebanon" Model Parlor Clock with Walnut Case

Gilbert, Wm. L., Clock Company:
Victorian Renaissance Revival walnut "Lebanon" model, the tall pointed fanned pediment w/roundel above a row of short turned spindles above stepped sides ending in curled-down ears w/roundels over the paneled arched tall door w/reeded molding, decorated w/a fancy silver stencil spider web & grass design below the brass bezel & large dial w/Roman numerals, brass pendulum w/embossed flowers & leaves, rectangular deep platform base w/sawtooth band, eight-day movement, time & strike, ca. 1890, 4 1/2 x 13 1/8", 20 1/2" h. $400-450

Wm. L. Gilbert Clock Company "Necho" Model Parlor Clock with Walnut Case

Gilbert, Wm. L., Clock Company: Walnut "Necho" model, a pointed scroll-carved pediment above scroll-cut & line-incised cornice above the rounded & reeded glazed door w/ornate silver stenciled drapery design over the large dial w/Roman numerals & a brass pendulum w/applied grape leaves, scroll cutouts at the lower sides above the flaring stepped base, eight-day movement, time, strike & alarm, ca. 1890, 5 x 13 1/4", 20 3/4" h. **$300-350**

*Wm. L. Gilbert
Clock Company
Parlor Clock
with Mahogany
Case*

**Gilbert, Wm. L.,
Clock
Company:**
Mahogany round-
top shelf clock,
ca. 1875, eight-
day, time &
strike, spring driven, 10 1/2" w., 17 1/2" h.. ....**$200**

Wm. L. Gilbert Clock Company Parlor Clock with Rosewood Case

Gilbert, Wm. L., Clock Company: Rosewood shelf clock, ca. 1860, spring driven, 13" w., 19 1/2" h. $250

Wm. L. Gilbert Clock Company Parlor Clock with Rosewood-Veneer Case

Gilbert, Wm. L., Clock Company: Rosewood-veneered shelf clock, ca. 1870-1880, eight-day, time, bell strike, & alarm.
....**$175**

E. Ingraham Parlor Clock with Walnut and Rosewood Case

Ingraham, E.: Walnut & rosewood shelf clock, patented Sept. 30, 1862, time & strike, 10 1/2" w., 14 1/2" h. **$425**

*Jerome &
Company
Parlor Clock
with Walnut
Case and
Ebony Trim*

Jerome & Company: Walnut shelf clock, ca. 1855, ebony trim, 30-hour, time & strike, 11 1/2" w., 16 1/2" h.. ....**$225**

F. Kroeber "Chalet" Model Parlor Clock with Walnut Case

Kroeber, F.: "Chalet" walnut parlor shelf clock, ca. 1887, pendulum cover removed to expose pendulum, eight-day, time & strike, 17 1/2" h. **$265**

F. Kroeber "Kansas" Model Parlor Clock with Walnut Case

Kroeber, F.: "Kansas" walnut parlor shelf clock, ca. 1881, carved drop & upright finials, eight-day, time & strike, 20" h.. ....$425

F. Kroeber "Occidental" Model Parlor Clock with Walnut Case

Kroeber, F.:
"Occidental" model, upright walnut case w/a molded arched top w/corner urn-form finials & a large central scroll & shell crest w/a carved head of classical woman in the center, tall front molded arch encloses the large brass bezel around the round white dial w/Roman numerals, the long glass panel below decorated w/stenciled scroll & geometric designs, all flanked by mirrored side panels & turned drop finials w/small quarter-round side shelves fitted w/gilt cast-metal figures of cupids, ovoid molded base w/a gilt cartouche on the front, round star-cut glass pendulum bob, eight-day time & strike movement, partial label on rear of case, replacement cupids, some wear to dial, ca. 1880, 24 1/2" h. $840

New Haven "Corsair" Model Parlor Clock with Oak Case

New Haven: "Corsair" oak shelf clock, eight-day, time, strike, & alarm, spring driven, 5" dial, 17" w., 23 1/2" h. **$900**

New Haven Parlor Clock with Rosewood-Veneer Case

New Haven: Rosewood-veneered shelf clock, 30-hour, time, strike, & alarm, spring driven, 9 1/2" w., 13 1/2" h...............**$195**

*New Haven "Elbe"
Model Parlor Clock
with Walnut Case*

New Haven: "Elbe" model, walnut case w/molded arching cornice featuring beading & urn-form decorations hanging from each side, leaf & scroll carved crest, rectangular body sits on stepped base w/urn-form side decorations sitting on square bases on each side, original painted dial w/Roman numerals, original tri-color glass panel in bottom, Gilbert patent indicator pendulum, eight-day time/strike/alarm movement, some flaking on dial, ca. 1880, 24" h. $280

Seth Thomas "Atlas" Model Parlor Clock with Walnut Case

Thomas, Seth: "Atlas" model, walnut case w/molded arched crest & corner ringed finials on pediment, three-quarter round ring-turned columns at each corner of body flank the door w/bronze decoration on glass over the white dial w/black Roman numerals, nickel-plated gong base & pendulum, cove molding to beveled rectangular base w/square wafer feet, original black label inside, eight-day time & strike movement, gong striking on the quarter hour, hour hand replaced, ca. 1886, 22 1/2" h. **$1,792**

Seth Thomas "Atlanta" Model Parlor Clock with Gilded Side Pillars

Thomas, Seth: "Atlanta" parlor shelf clock, side pillars w/gilt trim, eight-hour, time & strike, 12 1/2" w., 20" h. **$275**

Seth Thomas Stained-Case Parlor Clock with Incised Carving and Railing on Top

Thomas, Seth: Stained parlor shelf clock, ca. 1890, incised carving & railing on top, eight-day, time, strike, & alarm, 13" w., 21" h. **$450**

*Seth Thomas
Flat-Top Parlor
Clock with
Mahogany Case*

Thomas, Seth: Mahogany flat-top shelf clock, ca. 1866-1870 (Plymouth Hollow label), Geneva stops to prevent over-winding, eight-day, time & strike, 11 1/2" w., 15 1/2" h. **$200**

*E.N. Welch
"Dolaro"
Model Parlor
Clock with
Walnut Case*

Welch, E.N.: "Dolaro" walnut parlor shelf clock, ca. 1885, incised carving, eight-day, time, strike & alarm, 14" w., 22 1/2" h. **$350**

*E.N. Welch
Parlor
Clock with
Mahogany
Case*

Welch, E.N.: Mahogany shelf clock, patented 1868, 30-hour, time
& strike, spring driven, 10 1/2" w., 14" h. **$145**

E.N. Welch Victorian Eastlake-Style Parlor Clock with Walnut Case

Welch, E.N.: Victorian Eastlake-style walnut case, the high two-tier pediment w/a palmette top over a turned roundel flanked by reeded blocks & pierced designs, similar lower tier above the tall molded glazed door decorated w/ornate gilt stenciling over the dial w/Roman numerals, cut-out & line-incised side panels, wide reeded rectangular flat base, eight-day movement, time, strike & alarm, ca. 1890, 4 3/4 x 15 1/4", 24 1/2" h. **$350-400**

Welch, Spring & Company Victorian Renaissance Revival-Style Parlor Clock with Walnut Case

Welch, Spring & Company: Walnut case, Victorian Renaissance Revival style, peaked pediment w/dentil-cut crestrail centered by a block w/a carved classical bust above a molded cornice & a line-incised frieze above the arched, molded glazed door decorated w/a silver stenciled design of stalks of wheat & small desert & seascape vignettes, rectangular platform base w/flaring sides & line-incised decoration, dial w/Roman numerals, brass pendulum w/inset glass medallion, paper label on the back, eight-day movement, time & strike, ca. 1880, missing top finial, 5 x 13 1/2", 21" h. **$300-500**

Pillar-and-Scroll Clocks

Mark Leavenworh Pillar-and-Scroll Clock with Mahogany-Veneer and Stained-Hardwood Case

Leavenworth, Mark: Mahogany-veneered and stained-hardwoods pillar-and-scroll shelf clock, replaced brass finials, ivory escutcheon, ca. 1825; 30-hour, time and strike, weight driven; 16 1/2" w., 31" h. **$3,500**

Elisha Neal Pillar-and-Scroll Clock with Urn-Form Finials, Reverse-Painted Scene of Large House, and Short Tapered Feet

Neal, Elisha: Pillar-&-scroll-style, bonnet top w/three urn-form finials, body w/ two-panel glass door w/dial above & reverse-painted tablet at bottom showing large house set on extensive grounds within a fancy border, oval cut-out in center shows pendulum, body flanked by two slender ring-turned columns, base w/valanced skirt & short tapered feet, square dial w/black Arabic numerals, delicate spandrels & center ring, time & strike movement, new reverse painting, left foot replaced, small veneer repair on skirt, label w/some tears & a missing piece, ca. 1830, 31" h. **$2,016**

Eli Terry Pillar-and-Scroll Clock with Outside Escapement and Reverse-Painted Scene of House

Terry, Eli: Rare outside-escapement pillar-and-scroll clock, mahogany veneer on butternut secondary wood case, broken-scroll crest w/urn finial & matching smaller corner finials, slender ring-turned columns flanking door w/two old glass panes & original brass door turn, top pane over the dial w/black Roman numerals & delicate pale pink & green floral spandrels & cartouche w/decorations in similar colors, the lower pane w/metallic scalloped border around reverse-painted pastoral scene w/house, bordered oval window in center for pendulum, molded base w/ogee apron & slender tapered legs, top of door is stamped "XXI," original label, time & strike movement, lower pane repainted, left scroll cracked & repaired, tip of right scroll replaced, three mahogany wood finials old but probably replaced brass finials, edge of both dial stiffeners & inside of bottom door stretcher shaved, one section of the backboard behind the movement replaced, ca. 1817, 28 3/4" h. **$10,080**

*E. Terry & Sons
Pillar-and-Scroll
Clock with
Wooden Works and
Rosewood Case*

Terry, E. & Sons:
Rosewood pillar-
and-scroll shelf
clock, wooden
works, ca. 1818-
24; 30-hour, time and strike, weight driven; 17 1/2" w., 31" h.
....**$1,250**

Porcelain/China Clocks

Ansonia Clock with Dresden Porcelain Case

Ansonia: Dresden porcelain shelf clock, eight-day, time & strike, spring driven, 4 1/2" dial, 13" w., 12" h. **$550**

Ansonia Clock with Royal Bonn Porcelain Case and Open Escapement

Ansonia: Royal Bonn porcelain shelf clock w/open escapement, porcelain dial, eight-day, time & strike, 13 1/2" w., 15" h.
....**$1,250**

Ansonia Clock with Royal Bonn Porcelain Case and Open Escapement

Ansonia: Royal Bonn porcelain shelf clock, w/porcelain dial & open escapement, eight-day, time & strike, spring driven, 10 1/2" w., 11 1/2" h. $1,100

Ansonia "Cameo No. 1" Model Clock with Jasperware Ceramic Case

Ansonia: "Cameo No. 1" model, arched serpentine-sided German jasperware ceramic case in pale blue w/relief images of cherubs & floral garlands in white & relief scrolls in white forming the border, white porcelain dial w/black Roman numerals & beveled glass w/decorative brass bezel, 30-hour time-only movement, ca. 1901, 5" h...**$336**

*Ansonia
"Chemung"
Model Clock
with Porcelain
Case*

Ansonia: "Chemung" model, upright porcelain case w/arching top & serpentine sides, a wide decorative stamped brass bezel enclosing the round white dial featuring elaborate reticulated brass enclosing the black Arabic numerals, the case in white w/pink & gilt floral & scroll designs around the border & delicate pastel flowers in the area below the dial, on the top & sides, time & strike movement, heavy wear to gold trim, ca. 1910, 10 1/2" h. $336

Ansonia "Goblin" Model Clock with Royal Bonn China Case

Ansonia: "Goblin" model, Royal Bonn china case, high rounded case w/scrolls at top & down the sides continuing to form out-curved scroll feet, lime green shading to lighter green ground w/aster-like flowers in yellow, magenta, orange, gold & aqua, a decorative brass bezel enclosing the white dial w/Roman numerals, the decoration w/gilt highlighting, good Royal Bonn trademark, 30-hour time-only movement, dial pan loose in bezel, set stem missing, some loss of gold highlights, ca. 1904,6 1/4" h.
....**$336**

Ansonia "La Cannes" Model Clock with Royal Bonn China Case

Ansonia: "La Cannes" model, Royal Bonn china rectangular case w/decorative scrolling & floral crest above the porcelain dial within ornate notched brass bezel & center ring, white chapter ring w/Roman numerals & open escapement, on square feet, decorated in lime green at top shading to yellow in center to dark green at base, trimmed w/yellow & purple flowers painted in area under dial, Royal Bonn trademark, time & strike movement, ca. 1905, 11 3/4" h...**$1,064**

Ansonia "La Chappelle" Model Clock with Royal Bonn China Case

Ansonia: "La Chapelle" model, Royal Bonn china case in green & aqua w/h.p. deep pink roses underneath dial & on sides, crest formed by head of a woman in the Art Nouveau style w/flowing hair & floral wreath on her head, flanked by open scroll handles on upper sides, the bottom sides scrolling to form feet, all high-lighted w/molded floral & leaf decorations accented in gilt, Bonn trademark on rear of case, dial w/brass notched bezel, black Arabic numerals & open escapement, time & strike movement, ca. 1901, 12" h. **$1,960**

Ansonia "La Charny" Model Clock with Royal Bonn China Case

Ansonia: "La Charny" model, Royal Bonn china case, aqua at top, dark green at bottom shading to yellow around dial, yellow & pink water lilies on pond h.p. beneath dial, griffins scrolling at 45-degree angles at either side, griffin head crest, gilt accents, Royal Bonn trademark on rear of case, dial w/gold-tone beaded bezel, open escapement & black Roman numerals, time & strike movement, ca. 1905, 11 1/2" h. **$1,848**

Ansonia "La Claire" Model Clock with Royal Bonn China Case

Ansonia: "La Claire" model, Royal Bonn china case w/scroll-molded sides, apron & feet, urn-form finial, lime green & cream color overall w/gold accents, flowers painted in shades of pink & blue under dial, porcelain dial w/Arabic numerals & fancy gold bezel, time & strike movement, ca.1905, 15" h. **$1,540**

Ansonia "La Layon" Model Clock with Royal Bonn China Case

Ansonia: "La Layon" model, Royal Bonn china waisted case w/pink & yellow ground & pink & yellow roses & green leaves around dial, gilt scroll crest, S-scroll brackets on either side, four ribbed scroll feet, white dial w/brass notched bezel, black Roman numerals & original hands, time & strike movement, chip by right winding hole, ca. 1910, 14 1/2" h. **$1,792**

Ansonia "La Palma" Clock with Royal Bonn Case

Ansonia: "La Palma" model, Royal Bonn china rectangular case w/a molded arched top w/blossom crest, the porcelain glazed dial w/brass decorative bezel, white chapter ring w/black Arabic numerals & open escapement, the case w/a dark green border decorated w/bright yellow & gold flowers, the sides in the form of tree trunks entwined w/yellow blossoms, short leaf feet on square bases & fleur-de-lis in apron, the dial surround in shades of lime green, yellow & cream w/purple, pink & yellow & gold flowers, time & strike movement, dark hairlines on dial, wrong hands, mismarked "LaRita," ca. 1905, about 11 3/4" h.....................**$1,288**

Ansonia "La Vera" Model Clock with Royal Bonn Case

Ansonia: "La Vera" model, upright Royal Bonn china case w/an arched scroll-molded crest tapering down to open S-scrolls flanking the waisted center case & continuing to form wide front panels, the white porcelain dial within a beaded brass bezel, black Arabic numerals & open escapement in center, the case w/deep reddish purple scrolls & sides, the area around the dial decorated w/yellow daisies & purple violets, the top & sides w/further scroll & floral decoration, time & strike movement, Bonn trademark on rear, ca. 1901, 12 1/4" h..$3,016

Ansonia "La Vendee" Model Clock with Royal Bonn China Case

Ansonia: "La Vendee" model, Royal Bonn china case, a tall waisted upright case scrolling out widely at bottom to form feet, the porcelain dial w/a notched brass bezel & center ring, white chapter ring w/black Arabic numerals & open escapement, case sides w/cut-out loops at the top flanking an upright scrolled crest, teal blue top, the center & lower sides in shades of yellow & tan, a cluster of large pink & red poppies below the dial, all accented w/gilt, time & strike movement, ca. 1915, 14 1/2" h.

....$1,456

Ansonia "No. 411" Model Clock with China Case

Ansonia: "No. 411" model, domed china case w/ogee sides & slightly peaked crest, original round paper dial w/a decorative brass bezel & center, black Arabic numerals, case in forest green shading to cream under dial w/floral decorations of large white & pink blossoms, gold highlights, time & strike movement, replaced hands, dial darkened w/age, ca. 1910, 11" h. $672

Ansonia "La Mine" Model Clock with Royal Bonn China Case

Ansonia: Ornate Royal Bonn "La Mine" model china case, the tall upright arched case w/waisted sides molded at the top w/a central shell flanked by long open scrolls w/further scrolls down the sides & across the base w/incurved scroll feet, painted a deep magenta at the top w/pale yellow in the center shading to dark green at the base, decorated on the front w/large h.p. white & magenta blossoms & green leaves, the large brass bezel around the porcelain dial, Arabic numerals, open escapement, eight-day movement, time & strike, ca. 1900, 6 1/4 x 11", 13 1/2" h. **$1,000-1,200**

French Clock with Limoges China Case Featuring Columns and Classical Maiden Figurine

France: Limoges china case, slender upright form w/an ornate scroll-molded top surrounding the dial w/Arabic numerals & a seconds dial above the narrow waist w/molded columns flanking a center panel painted w/a classical maiden reaching up to a flower branch, scroll- & leaf-molded platform base, gilt trim, early 20th c., 12 1/2" h. **$1,210**

*New Haven Hanging
Wall Clock with
Porcelain Case*

New Haven: Porcelain hanging wall clock, patented July 1895, secondhand, eight-day, time only, 7" d. $300

New Haven Clock with Porcelain Case

New Haven: Porcelain small case shelf clock, 30-hour time only, spring driven, 6" w., 5" h. $75

New Haven "San Remo" Model Hanging Clock with Porcelain Case

New Haven: "San Remo" porcelain wall clock, one-day, time only, hair-spring driven, 2 1/2" dial, 9" w., 10" h. $375

New Haven Clock with Jasperware Case

New Haven: Shelf clock w/jasperware case, 30-hour, time only, spring driven, 5 1/2" w., 7" h. **$175**

Ansonia (Left), German (Center), and New Haven (Right) Clocks with Porcelain Cases

Various Manufacturers:
Ansonia:
(Left) Baby w/clock
German-made:
(Center) Colored green & white
New Haven:
(Right) Colored green & white, ca. 1900
6" to 8" height range..**$250 each**

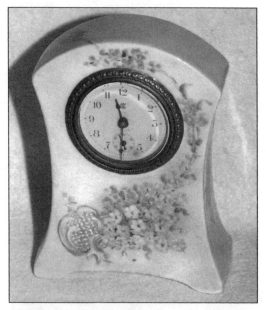

Waterbury Porcelain-Case Clock Decorated with Floral Design

Waterbury: Porcelain shelf clock w/floral design on case, 30-hour, time only, spring driven, 4" w., 6" h. **$175**

Pressed Oak Clocks

*Ansonia Clock
with Pressed
Oak Case*

Ansonia: Oak shelf clock, ca. 1880, pressed designs, eight-day, time & strike, 15" w., 23" h.. ....**$295**

W.L. Gilbert "Egypt" Model Clock with Pressed Oak Case

Gilbert, W.L.: "Egypt" oak shelf clock (part of the Egyptian series), pressed designs, eight-day, time & strike, 17" w., 25" h. **$300**

W.L. Gilbert "Mogul" Model Clock with Pressed Oak Case

Gilbert, W.L.: "Mogul" oak shelf clock (part of the Egyptian series), ca. 1895, pressed design, eight-day, time, strike & alarms, 16" w., 24" h. **$300**

W.L. Gilbert
"Pasha" Model
Clock with Pressed
Oak Case

Gilbert, W.L.: "Pasha" oak shelf clock (part of the Egyptian series), ca. 1905, pressed designs, eight-day, time, strike & alarm, 15 1/2" w., 25" h. **$300**

W.L. Gilbert "Pyramid" Model Clock with Pressed Oak Case

Gilbert, W.L.: "Pyramid" oak shelf clock (part of the Egyptian series), pressed designs, eight-day, time & strike, 15 1/2" w., 24" h. **$300**

W.L. Gilbert "Navy Number 27" Model Clock with Pressed Oak Case

Gilbert, W.L.: "Navy Number 27" pressed oak shelf clock, ca. 1880, eight-day, time & strike, spring driven, 15" w., 24" h.
....**$225**

*W.L.
Gilbert
Clock with
Pressed
Oak Case*

Gilbert, W.L.: Oak shelf clock, ca. 1901, pressed designs, eight-day, time & strike, 15 1/2" w., 23" h. **$245**

E. Ingraham Clock with Pressed Oak Case

Ingraham, E.: Oak shelf clock, pressed designs, eight-day, time, strike, & alarm, 15" w., 22" h. **$225**

E. Ingraham "Post" Model Clock with Pressed Oak Case

Ingraham, E.: "Post" model oak shelf clock, ca. 1910, incised designs and applied decorations, eight-day, time & strike, 15" w., 23" h. **$275**

New Haven Clock with Pressed Oak Case and Side Mirrors

New Haven: Oak shelf clock w/side mirrors, pressed designs, eight-day, time, strike & alarm, 16" w., 24" h.....................**$450**

*Sessions
Clock with
Pressed Oak
Case*

Sessions: Oak shelf clock, ca. 1880, pressed designs, eight-day time & strike, 15" w., 23" h.. ....**$300**

Statue/Figural Clocks

Ansonia Clock Company "Echo" Model Figural Alarm Clock with Nickel-Plated Case and Figure of Boy Holding Hammer Over Bell

Ansonia Clock Company: "Echo" model automaton, nickel-plated case w/cast figure of boy holding hammer & sitting next to bell set at an angle on cylindrical dial case, boy strikes bell w/hammer on the hour, dial w/Roman numerals on tiny ring-turned feet, 30-hour time & strike movement, some roughness on case, nickel plating on back worn, ca. 1880, 7 3/4" h. $1,960

Ansonia Clock Company "Music and Poetry" Figural Clock with Two Classical Female Figures and Cast-Metal Case

Ansonia Clock Company: "Music & Poetry" cast-metal case w/two standing classical female figures flanking the upright dial case topped by an ornate figural urn & raised on a square plinth, the white porcelain dial under beveled glass w/decorative brass bezel, center ring & original hands, open escapement & black Arabic numerals, all on a rectangular base w/gilt metal center & reticulated corner embellishments, one figure stands beside a small three-legged table, the other plays a harp, signed time & strike movement, dirty condition, black paint needs to be removed from metal, ca. 1894, 20 1/2" h. $1,456

Ansonia Clock Company "Opera" Model Figural Clock with Seated Classical Figure and Cast-Metal Case

Ansonia Clock Company: "Opera" model cast-metal case, the tapering rectangular base w/sawtooth apron & cast-metal scroll feet supporting a large cast-metal figure of a seated classical woman on an elaborate stool & holding a wreath w/a lyre at the side, the ornate upright cast-metal clock case to one side enclosing a brass bezel around the porcelain face w/Roman numerals, eight-day movement, time & strike, open escapement, minor surface wear, ca. 1885-95, 8 x 21", 16 1/4" h. **$800-1,000**

Bourdin Figural Clock with Bronze Sculptured Retriever and Black Marble Case

Bourdin (France): Black marble rectangular case w/molded pediment topped by bronze sculpture of retriever signed "P.J. Mene," a glass pane over the rectangular decorated gilt dial surround w/round time dial & two oblong dial cartouches w/two subsidiary dials each, all white w/black numerals/text, the time dial w/Roman numerals & subsidiary seconds dial, the panels containing dials w/days of the week, months & dates of the month & moon phases in Arabic numerals, dial signed "Bourdin, Hr. Bté, Rue de la Paix 28, a Paris," the beveled block base on short beveled feet, time & strike movement also signed "Bourdin, a Paris, Nr. 3802," small chip to marble, ca. 1880, 19" h. **$5,880**

French Art-Nouveau Figural Clock with Three Female Busts and Gilt-Metal Body

France: Art Nouveau, gilt-metal, the circular clock face w/black Arabic numerals surrounded by three fully sculpted female busts, each w/long hair & smiling, angular tapering base terminating in a quatrefoil foot, works impressed "Medaille d'Argent," ca. 1900, 10 1/2" h. **$977**

French "The Astronomer" Model Figural Clock with Rose-Garlanded Cherub and Bronze and Ormolu Case

France: "The Astronomer" figural clock, bronze & ormolu case, a cast & gilded round dial w/floral center & cast blossom bezel w/black Roman numerals & signed "LeRoy, Paris," raised atop a bronze column w/ormolu ribbon & fruit-filled urn trim, standing next to a rose-garlanded cherub standing beside a telescope & globe on columnar base, all atop a deep rectangular platform base w/a blossom & leaf band across the front, the beveled base molding on ornate triangular feet, silk thread time & strike movement bears number "123," some repairs, compass missing from figure's hand, ca. 1830, 14" h. **$2,520**

French Figural Clock with Bronzed Lioness and Red Marble Base

France: Bronzed metal, a large figural female lion w/a gilt-metal finish resting above a rockwork base inset w/a round clock w/an enameled porcelain dial w/Arabic numerals, all on a red marble rectangular platform w/small brass feet, late 19th c. **$360**

*French Figural Clock
with Spread-Winged
Eagle and Patinated
Cast-Metal Base*

France: Dark patinated
cast-metal case, the top
section w/wreath frame
enclosing the round white
porcelain dial w/black
Roman numerals & brass
bezel, dial raised on a
large metal ball enclosing
the movement & fitted
behind a large model of a spread-winged eagle perched on a
branch, ornately decorated base w/low scroll feet, eight-day platform lever time only, dust cover to movement missing, ca. 1890,
15 1/2" h. **$364**

French "The Sciences-Ingenuity Rewarded" Model Figural Clock with Two Standing Figures and Red Marble Base

France: Figural "The Sciences-Ingenuity Rewarded" model, two standing patinated spelter figures on rockwork & half-globe base, one figure holding lightning bolts aloft stands just below the other winged figure w/arm upraised, on a raised platform red marble base centered by the white dial w/gilt-metal scrolling bezel & black Arabic numerals, base on ornate gilt-spelter scroll feet & side scrolls, time & bell-strike movement, ca. 1900, 37" h. $1,568

French Lalique Glass "Le Jour et La Nuit" Figural Clock with Nude Male and Female and Wood Base

France: Lalique glass, "Le Jour et La Nuit," a large front greyish blue disk set upright on a high flaring wood base, the wide side molded on one side of the wide dial w/a nude male representing Day & on the other w/a nude female representing Night, the black central dial w/white Roman numerals, introduced in 1926, inscribed "R. Lalique France," 14 7/8" h. **$46,000**

French "La Terre" Model Figural Clock with Bronzed Female and Child Figures and Red Marble Base

France: "La Terre" statue clock, the top w/a bronzed spelter female figure of "Peace" standing next to a child sitting on a short column, she holds a gilt dove in her right hand while her raised left arm supports a bracket-mounted 4" globe made by E. Bertaux, Rue Serpente 25, Paris, all set atop a stepped rectangular base of variegated light violet marble, the front panel set w/a round white decorated porcelain dial w/an ornate brass bezel & black Arabic numerals, raised on ornate gilt-metal scroll feet, time & strike movement that strikes the hours & halves on a bell, ca. 1900, 29" h. **$2,240**

German Figural Clock with Large Spread-Winged Eagle Atop Rockwork Base

Germany: Cast spelter, figural case, a large spread-winged eagle atop a rockwork base enclosing a round brass bezel & small dial w/Arabic numerals, late 19th - early 20th c., 6 x 8 3/4", 13 1/2" h. **$250-300**

New Haven Clock Company "Bernard Pallisy" Model Figural Clock with Man Seated at Table on Cast-Iron Base

New Haven Clock Company: "Bernard Palisy" model, figural w/a cast metal gold-painted figure of a bearded man in Renaissance dress sitting on a stool at a round table w/spool base & reading papers, the upright clock next to figure w/an ornate gold-painted metal case w/footed notched disk-shaped crest w/C-scroll side handles & finial, hanging side decorations, outscrolled decorated base, the white porcelain dial w/brass bezel & center ring, beveled glass & black Arabic numerals, all on a black cast-iron rectangular base w/cast metal gilt leaf-form feet & front scroll decoration w/mask, eight-day time & strike movement, ca. 1900, 16" h. **$420**

Raingo Freres Louis XVI-Style Figural Clock with Figure of Reclining Woman on White Marble Base

Raingo Freres (Paris, France): Louis XVI-style white marble oblong case topped w/bronze figure of a reclining woman in draped robes looking at a branch of gilded leaves she holds in her hand, the body of the case w/panels decorated w/gilt bronze ornamentation, the center round dial bordered w/gilt swags & wreaths flanked by bronze figures of children, one reading a book, the other holding a globe, the white porcelain signed dial w/cobalt blue Roman numerals & finely chased & gilded hands, original signed time & strike movement w/silk thread suspension & count wheel strike on a bell, minor repairs to dial, ca. 1830, 20" h. $4,480

Seth Thomas & Sons Company "Pattern #8228 'The Flautist'" Model Figural Clock with Seated Female Figure and Gilt-Metal Case

Thomas, Seth, & Sons Company: "Pattern #8228 'The Flautist'" model, gilt-metal case, the top set w/a tall figure of a woman in classical robes sitting in a chair & holding a flute, the central case enclosing the signed dial w/brass bezel & black Roman numerals, the case sides flaring toward the base & embellished w/applied masks on sides & scroll design on front all flanked by serpents whose bodies scroll downward, the rectangular stepped-out case base tapering in at the sides & raised on scroll & block feet, time & strike round movement, hands replaced, ca. 1875, 18" h.
....**$560**

Steeple Clocks

M.W. Atkins & Company
Steeple Clock with
Rosewood-Veneer Front and
Mahogany-Veneer Sides

Atkins, M.W., & Company:
Steeple style, case w/rose-
wood-veneered front &
mahogany-veneered sides,
flat base, original Fenn faux
acid etch-style glass on front, white dial w/raised Roman numerals
& chapter ring, original label, OG-style movement w/curved riveted
extensions to extend plates & convert to an eight-day spring-driven
movement, some veneer loss, replaced hour hand, ca. 1848,
19 3/4" h. **$515**

Birge & Fuller Double-Steeple Clock with Mahogany and Mahogany-Veneer Case and Open Escapement

Birge & Fuller: Double-steeple style, mahogany & mahogany veneer, the peaked case w/pointed corner finials & half-round columns flanking the peaked door over the dial w/Roman numerals & a small reverse-painted lower glazed panel flanked by another pair of pointed finials above the stepped-out lower case w/a single long rectangular glazed door reverse-painted w/a bunch of fruits & leaves, on small button feet, eight-day "wagon spring" driven movement, minor imperfections, 1840s, 4 x 13 1/8", 27" h. **$3,105**

Birge & Fuller Double-Steeple Clock with Mahogany-Veneer Case

Birge & Fuller: Double-steeple model, simple molded mahogany-veneer case w/three-quarter round peaked columns, two flanking the upper peaked two-pane glass door, the upper pane over the original dial w/black Roman numerals & open escapement, the lower narrow rectangular pane w/a reverse-painted decoration of stylized leaf designs in greens & grays, the stepped-out lower section w/two finials & columns flanking a similar larger glass pane decorated w/a wreath design reverse-painted in white, green & gold, eight-day "wagon spring" time & strike, knob feet, signed movement, some veneer loss, some loose pieces, label not legible, dial repainted, ca. 1848, 27 1/2" h. **$3,360**

Chauncey Boardman Mirror-Tablet Steeple Clock with Mahogany-Veneer Case

Boardman, Chauncey: Mahogany-veneer mirror-tablet steeple clock, ca. 1845, 30-hour, reverse fusee movement, time & strike, 10" w., 20" h. **$400**

J.C. Brown Steeple Clock with Full-Ripple Onion-Top Case

Brown, J.C.: Full-ripple onion-top case w/three-quarter round ring-turned columns at four corners topped by slender knobbed & spired finials, molded base, two-pane glass door, top pane over the round dial w/ripple surround & black Roman numerals, bottom square pane w/original heart-shaped etched & cut design, eight-day time & strike movement, signature rubbed off dial, label missing some pieces, ca. 1848, 19 3/4" h. **$3,808**

*J.C. Brown
Steeple Clock
with Rosewood
Case*

Brown, J.C.: Rosewood steeple clock, time & strike, ca. 1850,
10" w., 19 1/2" h. **$400**

J.C. Brown
Steeple Clock
with Ripple-
Front Rosewood
Case

Brown, J.C.: Rosewood ripple-front steeple shelf clock, ca. 1855, time & strike, 10" w., 20" h..**$1,650**

Burroughs Clock Company Miniature Onion-Top Steeple Clock with Cherry Case

Burroughs Clock Company: Cherry miniature rounded steeple or onion-top clock, ca. 1870-1874, 5" w., 7" h. **$125**

W.L. Gilbert Steeple Clock with Mahogany-Veneer Case

Gilbert, W.L.: Mahogany-veneered steeple clock, ca. 1870, 30-hour, time & strike, spring driven..**$165**

W.L. Gilbert Miniature Steeple Clock with Walnut Case

Gilbert, W.L.: Miniature steeple-type clock, walnut case w/pointed pediment flanked by turned finials above the pointed two-pane glazed door, the upper pane opening to the white metal dial w/Roman numerals & painted spandrels, the lower panel w/a reverse-painted windmill scene, flat base, possibly a salesman's sample, eight-day time & strike movement, mid-19th c., 4 1/2 x 6 1/2", 10 3/4" h. **$250**

*W.L. Gilbert
Miniature
Steeple Clock
with Walnut
Case*

Gilbert, W.L.:
Miniature wal-
nut steeple case, a Gothic-arch frame flanked by simple columns
w/small metal spires, a round dial w/Roman numerals above a
square molding around a glass pane over a print of Victorian
women, back of case w/paper label reading "No. 52T English
Lancet," original finish, time only, 19th c., 2 1/4 x 4 3/4",
7" h...$70

Hamilton-Sangamo Corporation Electric Steeple Clock with Mahogany Case

Hamilton-Sangamo Corporation: Electric steeple clock, pointed mahogany case w/pointed finials flanking the two-pane pointed door, the upper pane over the dial w/Roman numerals & h.p. floral spandrels, the lower pane w/a reverse-painted landscape, flat molded base, revival of a 19th c. style clock, ca. 1940, 4 7/8 x 9 1/2", 14 3/4" h. $150-175

*Elisha Manross
Steeple Clock
with Rosewood
Case*

Manross, Elisha: Rosewood steeple shelf clock, 30-hour, time & strike, 10" w., 20" h. **$250**

*Elisha Manross
Steeple Clock with
Mahogany Case*

Manross, Elisha:
Steeple-style
mahogany case, two-
pane glazed door, top
pane over the white
dial w/Roman numer-
als, a frosted-glass
tablet in bottom pane
w/picture of hot air
balloon, clean label,
30-hour time & strike
movement, hands not
original, ca. 1850,
19 3/4" h. $476

New Haven
"Jerome" Model
Steeple Clock with
Rosewood Case

New Haven: "Jerome" rosewood steeple clock, eight-day, time & strike, spring driven, 4 1/2" dial, 10" w., 19" h. **$150**

New Haven Steeple Clock with Oak Case

New Haven: Oak steeple clock, eight-day, time & strike, spring driven, 9 1/2" w., 15 1/2" h. **$175**

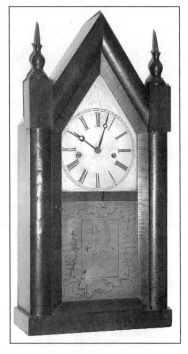

*Terryville
Manufacturing
Company Steeple Clock
with Rosewood Case*

**Terryville
Manufacturing
Company:** Rosewood
steeple-style case w/two-
pane glazed door, upper
pane over the white dial
w/Roman numerals, the
lower pane decorated
w/an etched center rec-
tangular scene of a foun-
tain framed by scrolls,
clean label, 30-hour time & strike movement features springs
behind the backplate, some restoration, tips on steeples have been
replaced, ca. 1855, 19 1/2" h..**$308**

Waterbury Clock Company Steeple Clock with Mahogany-Veneer Case

Waterbury Clock Company: Mahogany-veneer steeple clock, pointed top flanked by turned tapering finials above a pointed two-pane glazed door, the top pane over the dial w/Roman numerals, the replaced pane w/a frosty & etched leafy vine design, half-round columns down the sides, stepped base, one finial replaced, eight-day movement, strike & alarm, ca. 1860-80, 4 3/8 x 11 1/4", 19 1/4" h. **$250-300**

*E.N. Welch
Steeple Clock with
Mahogany Case*

Welch, E.N.: Mahogany steeple shelf clock, time, strike, & alarm, 10" w., 19 1/2" h. **$300**

Swinging-Arm Clocks

Ansonia "Arcadia" Model Swinging-Arm Clock Finished with Standing Maiden on Circular Base

Ansonia: "Arcadia" swing statue or figural clock, factory finished in bronze & nickel, originally made for jewelry store windows as attention getters, eight-day, time only, 4 1/2" dial, 3 1/2" h. **$5,000**

*Ansonia "Fortuna" Model
Swinging-Arm Clock with
Seated Maiden on
Circular Base*

Ansonia: "Fortuna" swing statue or figural clock, original bronze finish w/gilt pendulum, eight-day, time, 4 1/2" dial, 30" h. **$5,500**

Ansonia "Gloria" Model Swinging-Arm Clock of Winged Figure on Circular Base

Ansonia: "Gloria" swing statue or figural clock, barbedienne bronze finish, gold numbers on dial & gilded pendulum, eight-day, time, 4 1/2" w., 28 1/2" h. **$5,500**

Ansonia Swinging-Arm Clock of Classical Maiden Figure on Socle Base

Ansonia: Figural, a tall, bronzed-metal figure of a classical maiden on a socle base holding aloft in one hand the clock w/a brass bezel & ribbon crest over the round dial w/Arabic numerals suspending the bar-form pendulum w/stamped brass bob, clock & works swings w/the pendulum, ca. 1880s, 28" h. **$3,640**

Ansonia "Fisher Swing" Model Swinging-Arm Clock with Figure in Renaissance Attire on Stepped Circular Base

Ansonia: "Fisher Swing" model, bronze figure of a man in Renaissance attire, one arm raised to hold the large brass-framed dial & long pendulum, the dial w/Roman numerals, brass bezel & ribbon crest, further brass scrolls at the top of the three-bar pendulum ending in an ornate bob w/a stamped classical portrait bust, on stepped circular base, time-only movement, some discoloration to dial, ca. 1883, 22" h. $3,696

*Ansonia "Huntress Swing" Model
Swinging-Arm Clock with Figure of
Standing Woman in Clinging Gown
on Stepped Molded Base*

Ansonia: "Huntress Swing" model,
gold patinated metal figure of a
standing woman in clinging gown
w/raised left arm holding aloft the
brass-framed dial w/original white
paper face w/Roman numerals &
brass bezel, gilt-brass ribbon scroll
trim around dial & above the long
three-bar brass pendulum & bob
decorated w/a stamped bust portrait, on a stepped round molded
base, time-only movement, ca.
1883, 25" h. **$3,808**

Ansonia "Juno Swing" Model Swinging-Arm Clock with Classically Attired Figure on Embossed Waisted Pedestal

Ansonia: "Juno Swing" model, brass, figure of woman in classical dress standing on embossed waisted pedestal on circular base, the right arm holding a baton, the left raised to hold the ball dial w/decorative articulated crest & brackets & Arabic numerals suspending the bar-form pendulum w/orb-shaped bob w/drop finial, original patina, some pitting, dirt & oxidation, ca. 1895, 28 1/2" h. $3,864

Ansonia Swinging-Arm Clock with Figure of Art Nouveau Maiden Standing on Rockwork Base

Ansonia: Patinated cast metal, a figure of an Art Nouveau maiden standing on rockwork & holding the swinging clock up w/one arm, late 19th c., 24" h. $3,250

French Swinging-Arm Clock with Figure of Woman in Diaphanous Robes and Flowing Hair on Base with Brass Plaque

France: Bronzed spelter figure of "Brise d'Automne" (Autumn Breeze), a standing woman in diaphanous robes & flowing hair, on circular stepped wooden base painted to simulate marble, her upraised left arm holding the dial piece, the dial on 6" d. forest green ball trimmed w/gilt ribbon & scroll decoration, gilt hands & Roman numerals, long pendulum w/orb-shaped bob, statue & brass plaque on base signed "Moreau," time-only movement, ball professionally refinished, minute hand repaired, ca. 1890, 38 1/2" h..................**$4,760**

*French "Fluted Pillar" Model
Swinging-Arm Clock with
Wooden Pillar on Rectangular
Linden Wood Base*

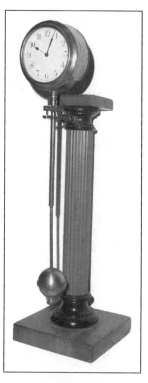

France: "Fluted Pillar" model, rectangular linden wood base supporting a wooden fluted pillar w/cast-metal capital & base, rectangular wood pediment supports the round brass clock w/a round white dial w/black Arabic numerals, slender straight brass rod pendulum holds the ringed orb bob, time-only movement, ca. 1915, 11" h. $1,232

French Swinging-Arm Clock with Figure of Woman in Draped Attire on White Marble and Scrolled-Foot Base

France: Gilt-spelter figure of a standing woman in draped attire w/right arm raised to hold the unframed 7" d. glass white dial w/gold leaf Roman numerals & hands & marked "Robert Houdin - Paris," the long open bar pendulum ending in a dark orb decorated w/gilt decoration & stars enclosing the movement, the movement suspended by a normal suspension spring w/a separate miniature gravity movement in the center of the glass dial w/a tiny pendulum & ratchet that advance the hands w/each swing of the arm, all atop a rectangular white marble base raised on a scalloped gilt-metal frame w/scroll feet, old crack near base of statue, professionally restored, ca. 1880, 24 1/2" h. $14,560

Japanese Swinging-Arm Clock with Brass Figure of Classical Woman on Black Plastic Base

Japan: Brass & spelter, a tall brass figure of a classical woman holding up the dial & swinging pendulum in one arm, on a black plastic base, a copy of a late Victorian design, ca. 1960s, 13 3/4" h. $200

Junghans "Barmaid" Model Swinging-Arm Clock with Figure of Barmaid on Stepped Circular Base

Junghans (Germany):
"Barmaid" model, metal figure of barmaid w/a ribbon in her hair wearing a low-cut blouse w/sleeves pushed up, skirt falling to just below knees & short, puffy overskirt, standing w/left hand on hip & holds clock in her extended right hand, the round brass clock case w/ribbon crest & scroll decoration under the dial encloses a white dial w/black Arabic numerals, a multi-rod brass pendulum & spherical brass bob, on a stepped circular base, original patina, time-only movement, gilt polished off clock case, ca. 1910, 13 1/2" h...**$1,680**

Junghans "Batboy" Model Swinging-Arm Clock with Figure of Boy Holding Bat on Oblong Base

Junghans (Germany): "Batboy" model, cast patinated-metal figure of a standing barefoot boy wearing rolled-up pants & undervest, holding short bat in his right hand & the clock in his upraised left hand, ornate brass case enclosing the white porcelain dial w/black Arabic numerals, brass bezel, multi-bar pendulum w/spiked orb bob, on oblong base, original dark greenish bronze patina, time-only movement, ca. 1910, 18" h. $2,016

Junghans Swinging-Arm Clock with Figure of Kangaroo on Rectangular Base

Junghans (Germany): Cast metal figure of a kangaroo standing on hind legs & holding clock arm in its mouth, brass case w/ribbon crest encloses the white dial w/black Arabic numerals, multibar brass pendulum w/spiked ringed orb bob, time-only movement, ca. 1910, 12" w. x 12" h. **$2,576**

*Junghans "Onion Boy" Model
Swinging-Arm Clock with Figure
of Boy Carrying Onions on
Circular Base*

Junghans (Germany): "Onion Boy" model, bronze-finished cast-spelter figure of a barefoot boy w/rolled up pants holding bunch of onions over left shoulder & holding clock in his upraised right hand, brass clock case w/ornate decoration at top & bottom of white porcelain dial w/black Arabic numerals, single-shaft pendulum tapering to spiked ringed orb bob, time-only movement, some wear, ca. 1900, 15 1/2" h.....................**$1,456**

Junghans "Onyx Pillar" Model Swinging-Arm Clock with Green Onyx Column, Ladder-Style Pendulum, and Circular Green Onyx Base

Junghans (Germany): "Onyx Pillar" model, brass clock case attached to a green onyx column w/rings of gilt spelter, case w/ribbon crest & floral decoration beneath dial, brass bezel enclosing the white dial w/black Arabic numerals, ladder-style brass pendulum w/ringed orb bob, circular green onyx base, time-only movement, ca. 1900, 10" h. **$1,568**

Tambour Clocks

W.L. Gilbert Tambour Clock with Oak Case

Gilbert, W.L.: Oak tambour mantel clock, ca. 1880, time & strike, 9 1/2" h. **$110**

E. Ingraham Miniature Tambour Clock with Wooden Case

Ingraham, E.: Miniature (baby camel back) wooden tambour mantel clock, metal dial, 8 1/2" w., 5 1/2" h. **$85**

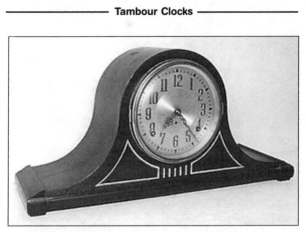

Plymouth Clock Company Tambour Clock with Wooden Case

Plymouth Clock Company: Wooden tambour mantel clock, eight-day, time & strike, 19" w., 9 1/2" h. **$125**

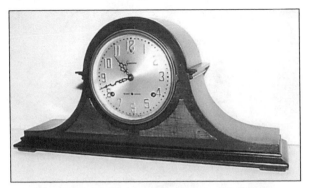

Sessions Tambour Clock with Mahogany Case and Westminster Chimes

Sessions: Mahogany tambour mantel clock, eight-day, time & strike. Westminster chimes, patented 1929, 18" w., 17 1/2" h. $175

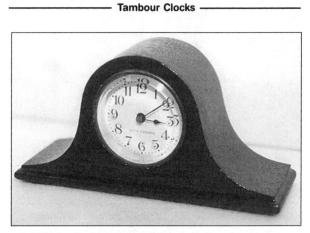

Seth Thomas Tambour Clock with Wooden Case

Thomas, Seth: Wooden case tambour mantel clock, 6 1/2" w., 3 1/2" h. **$85**

Seth Thomas Tambour Clock with Rosewood-Finish Case

Thomas, Seth: Adamantine (rosewood finish) tambour mantel clock, eight-day, time & strike, 17 1/2" w., 10 1/2" h. **$245**

Two- and Three-Deck Clocks

Seth Thomas Two-Deck Clock with Mahogany-Veneer Classical-Style Case and Elaborate Gilt Decorations

Thomas, Seth: Classical-style two-deck decorated mahogany-veneer case, the deep OG blocked top above large gilt-decorated half-round columns flanking the tall two-pane door, the upper pane over the dial w/Roman numerals, the lower pane decorated w/elaborate reverse-painted gilt decor of a scalloped frame enclosing lattice centered by a colored urn of flowers, the deep lower case w/heavy ogee scrolls flanking a small glazed door reverse-painted w/further gilt stencil decoration centering a diamond & bowl of colored flowers, flat base, dated 1863, eight-day movement, time & strike, original finish, 5 1/8 x 18 1/2", 32 1/2" h. **$1,200-1,500**

Birge, Peck & Company Triple-Deck Clock with Gilt Spread-Winged Eagle Splat and Star Designs on Lower Two Panes

Birge, Peck & Company: Triple-deck style, gilt spread-winged eagle splat flanked by rectangular molded-top chimneys w/molded circular decorations above gilt & faux finish ring-turned columns flanking the door w/three glass panes, top pane over the original square dial w/black Roman numerals, original hands & delicate spandrels of red flowers & green ferns, middle pane w/deep aqua border around gray, silver, green, cream & red design w/star motif, the bottom pane w/green border around gray, silver, green & cream floral design, the base w/gilt knob feet, eight-day time & strike strap brass movement, original weights & pendulum, clean label, some cracks in eagle, chip missing from chimney, paint loss to dial, ca. 1855, 36 1/2" h...**$2,688**

*C. & L.C. Ives
Three-Deck
Clock with
Walnut Case
and Painted
Scenes on
Lower Two
Panes*

Ives, C. & L. C.: Walnut triple-decker shelf clock, ca. 1830, time and strike, weight driven, 38" h. $700

Wag-on-the-Wall Clocks

French Pinwheel-Type Wag-on-the-Wall Clock with Convex Dial, Large Reeded Brass Pendulum and Large Round Bob

France: Pinwheel type, a round white porcelain convex dial w/engine-turned brass bezel, black Roman numerals & sweep seconds hand above the large reeded brass pendulum w/large round bob, eight-day time-only weight & pendulum movement, ca. 1860, 52" h. **$1,904**

German Wag-on-the-Wall Clock with Full-Color Scene of Village and Pendulum Engraved with Image of Horse

Germany: Flat decorated metal shield-shaped dial w/red & gold-leaf trim & full-color scene of village above dial, the round dial w/raised chapter ring & black Roman numerals, period hands, pendulum engraved w/image of horse, 30-hour time & strike movement, strike hammer improperly replaced but functioning, ca. 1860, 14" h. $420

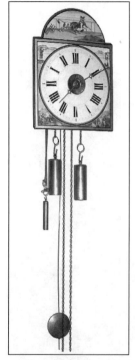

German Wag-on-the-Wall Clock with Scene of Bullfighter and Images of Children at Play

Germany: Square-dial plate w/arched top, the arch painted w/a polychrome scene of a bullfighter being gored by bull, the spandrels around the round dial decorated w/polychrome images of children at play, the dial w/heavy black Roman numerals & a stamped brass center ring & brass hands, brass weights & pendulum, 30-hour time/strike/alarm movement, ca. 1900, 13 1/2" h. **$392**

André Spéth Brass Wag-on-the-Wall Clock with Arched Cornice and Large Ornate Stamped Pendulum

Spéth, André (France): Embossed brass, the square upper section w/a sheet steel frame w/an arched stamped brass cornice, the open enameled dial w/Roman numerals signed "André Spéth à la Charité," the large long tapering rounded pendulum of ornate stamped brass w/C-scrolls, flowers & a classical urn, the dial w/hairlines & yellowed repair, w/weights & key, wrought-iron shelf a late replacement, late 18th - early 19th c., overall 56" h. $935

Wall Regulator Clocks

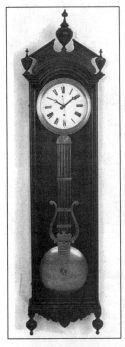

Ansonia Clock Company "Regulator No. 4" Model Wall Regulator Clock with Walnut Renaissance Revival-Style Case, Lyre-Form Pendulum, and Large Brass Bob

Ansonia Clock Company: "Regulator No. 4," walnut Renaissance Revival-style long case, the broken arch pediment w/a large turned central urn finial & smaller turned corner finials above an arched glazed front over a large round dial w/wide brass bezel & Roman numerals suspending a large brass pendulum w/a band of thin strings continuing into a lyre design above the large brass disk pendulum bob, molded base w/pointed scalloped apron & turned corner drops, ca. 1880. ....$5,880

*Atkins Clock Company
Wall Regulator Clock with
Rosewood Case and
Square Glass Tablet with
Gilt Center Decoration*

Atkins Clock Company: Drop regulator style, rosewood case, large round molded top around the white dial w/Roman numerals & original moon hands, the drop case w/a square glass tablet w/gilt center decoration on black background, eight-day time & strike movement, label, veneer chip, repainted dial, tablet replaced long ago, ca. 1865, 24 1/2" h. **$672**

Austrian One-Weight Wall Regulator Clock with Walnut Case, Arched Pediment, and Stepped Base with Drop Finial

Austria: One-weight model, tall walnut case w/molded arched pediment w/two finials, tall arched glass front over the brass bezel & white porcelain dial w/Roman numerals, a single small cylindrical brass weight & long pendulum w/a large brass bob, stepped base w/drop finial, time-only movement, replacement finials, spider web in porcelain dial, ca. 1890, 43 1/2" h. **$840**

Austrian Wall Regulator Clock with Walnut Case Accented with Dark Colored Blocks and Topped with Urn-Form Finials

Austria: Tall light walnut case w/molded pediment arching at center, urn-form center & corner finials & rectangular black panel accents, three-quarter round reeded columns at sides w/ring-turned capitals & bases flanking the tall arched glass door showing the round dial w/brass bezel & center ring, black Roman numerals & cut-out hands above the weights & pendulum, the base w/an ogee drop w/ringed knob finial & conforming corner finials, the case accented w/blocks of dark color, door warp caused cracking in the glass, ca. 1880, 53" h. **$952**

Austrian Wall Regulator Clock with Walnut Case and Crest with Carved Eagle

Austria: Walnut case, the high arched crest centered by a carved relief eagle above a flaring stepped cornice above the tall case w/a glazed front panel over the round dial w/Arabic numerals & the long two-weight pendulum w/large brass bob, the panel flanked by columnar sides w/urn-turned supports on blocks, molded base w/tapering ogee paneled drop w/finial, ca. 1880, 6 x 16 1/4", 46" h. **$840**

Austrian Wall Regulator Clock with Walnut Case, High Scroll-Cut Crest, and Shell Carving

Austria: Walnut case, the high scroll-cut crest w/a flat top over a shell carving flanked by corner blocks w/turned urn finials above a molded cornice over a long glazed panel showing the round dial w/Roman numerals & the long wooden pendulum w/large brass bob, the side columns w/ring- & knob-turned top & bottom sections centered by a narrow reeded colonette, ogee molded fluted base drop w/finial flanked by corner drop finials, ca. 1880, 7 x 16 1/2", 48" h. **$728**

Gustav Becker One-Weight Wall Regulator Clock with Viennese-Style Walnut Case and Arched Pediment

Becker, Gustav (Germany): Tall walnut case in Viennese style, arched pediment above the arched glass door w/molded frame over the white dial w/black Arabic numerals, a brass bezel, center ring, weight, pendulum & bob, ogee base drop w/beveled drop finial, one-weight time-only movement signed w/Becker's medal of honor seals, ca. 1895, 44" h. **$504**

Gustav Becker Three-Weight Wall Regulator Clock with Ornately Carved Crest of Scrolls, Columns, and Mask

Becker, Gustav (Germany): Tall wooden case w/molded pediment w/band of geometric carving topped w/a high, ornately carved crest w/scrolls, columns & mask, the tall arched glass door flanked by three-quarter round reeded columns w/ring-turned tops & Ionic-type capitals & turned baluster-form bottoms on rectangular bevel-carved bases, the dial w/silver chapter ring w/black Arabic numerals, simple brass bezel & center ring, the dial, weights & pendulum bob all w/matching scroll engraving, the molded & carved base drop w/incised decoration, three-weight time, strike & chime movement strikes grand sonnerie sequence on two steel rods, carved top is new, bottom finial missing, chapter ring w/some oxidation, bezel loose, ca. 1890, 46" h. $1,400

Chelsea Clock Company "No. 1 Pendulum" Model Wall Regulator Clock with Oak Case and Large Round Molding Surrounding the Dial

Chelsea Clock Company: "No. 1 Pendulum" model, long oak case w/a large round top molding enclosing the white dial w/black Roman numerals, the long rectangular drop case w/a glass door over the pendulum & large brass bob, short cove-molded base drop, time-only movement signed w/Chelsea trademark & "A-142," dial repainted, movement restrung, ca. 1920, 34" h. **$1,568**

*Eastman Clock Company
"Pendulum No. 1" Model Wall
Regulator Clock with Oak Case,
Red and Black Painted Glass
Panel, and Large Round Molding
Surrounding the Dial*

Eastman Clock Company:
"Pendulum No. 1" model, oak
case w/large round molding surrounding the white dial w/black
Roman numerals & marked "Daniel Pratt's Son, Boston, Mass,"
drop case w/molding surrounding a red & black painted glass
panel, signed eight-day weight movement, some flaking on dial,
weight baffle w/crack, ca. 1895, 33" h. **$1,792**

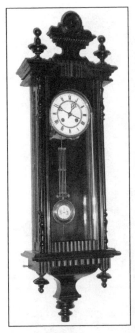

German Wall Regulator Clock with Ebonized Wood Case, High Center Crest with a Roundel, and Large Ring-Turned Corner Finials

Germany: Long rectangular ebonized wood case w/a flaring stepped cornice supporting a high center crest w/a roundel over flaring molding & large ring-turned corner finials, two three-quarter round colonettes w/baluster-form tops & bottoms flank the tall arched glass front w/a brass bezel & white round porcelain dial w/Roman numerals, the multi-rod pendulum w/a brass ring bezel enclosing a white plaque printed w/"R-A," molded base over a ribbed band & long ogee base drop w/drop finial flanked by corner drop finials, eight-day spring time & strike movement, some restoration, ca. 1890, 37" h...$504

*German Miniature
Cuckoo Clock-Style
Wall Regulator Clock
in Walnut Case with
Peaked Top*

Germany: Miniature
Black Forest-type in an
ornately carved walnut
cuckoo clock-style
case w/peaked top
overhanging cut-out
fruit & leaf decorations
vining around sides &
base, half-round
columns flanking arch-
topped glazed door
w/more vine decora-
tion over the white
porcelain dial w/mold-
ed brass bezel & center ring & black Roman numerals, a brass
three-bar pendulum w/a brass ring-form bob inset w/a porcelain
plaque lettered "R - A," extensions of side columns form drop
finials a fluted horizontal base rail also w/turned end finials &
square blocks w/roundels, needs a 00 key but crank works,
replacement hands, missing small carved rail of leaves on top,
ca. 1890, 12" h. **$1,792**

German One-Weight Viennese-Style Wall Regulator Clock with Walnut-Veneer Case Topped by Arched Cornice and Three Turned Finials

Germany: One-weight regulator in the Viennese style, long walnut veneer case w/arched cornice & three turned finials, the base w/narrow reeded pilasters w/scroll-carved brackets at the top & base corners flanking the tall glass front over a brass bezel & white dial w/Roman numerals, single weight & long pendulum w/large brass bob, base tapering center drop & three drop finials, original time only movement, drop finial switched to top at some point, other five finials replaced, ca. 1880, 44" h. **$840**

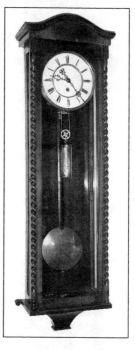

German One-Weight Wall Regulator Clock with Rosewood Case, Barley Twist Columns, and Stepped Arched Top

Germany: Rosewood case w/barley twist columns, stepped arched top, drop finial, white dial w/Roman numerals, one weight, eight-day time-only movement w/dead beat escapement, some veneer loss, hairline cracks to chapter ring, dial chipped, ca. 1870, 38" h. **$784**

Wm. L. Gilbert "Regulator No. 10" Model Wall Regulator Clock with Oak Case and Molded Pediment and Cornice

Gilbert, Wm. L.: "Regulator No. 10" model, long oak case w/molded pediment & cornice w/molding above a panel carved w/ribs & a scallop design above the round white dial w/metal bezel & black Roman numerals & subsidiary seconds dial, wood molding below the dial & over a long glass pane showing the pendulum & brass pendulum bob, the molded drop w/semicircular carved sides, time-only movement, missing seven oak balls at top, some nicks & scrapes to weight, ca. 1895, 52 1/2" h. **$5,880**

*E. Howard & Company "Regulator No.
9" Model Wall Regulator Clock with
Walnut Figure 8-Shaped Case and
Molded Bullseye Finial*

Howard, E. & Company: "Regulator
No. 9" model, walnut figure 8-shaped
case w/molded bullseye finial over
molded round frame around the white
signed dial w/black Roman numerals,
the midsection w/glass panel
w/beveled frame & reverse-painted
border in black & gilt conforming to
waist, the gilt pendulum stick showing
through center, the lower circular
glass panel w/reverse-painted concentric circles of black, gilt &
deep red, w/pendulum bob showing through center, base drop
finial, time-only movement, weight & baffle replaced, ca. 1910,
37" h. **$9,240**

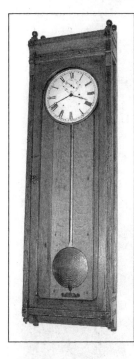

E. Howard & Company "Regulator No. 89" Model Wall Regulator Clock with Oak Case, Concave-Front Cornice, and Arched Glass Panel

Howard, E. & Company: "Regulator No. 89" model, simple rectangular oak case w/four corner knob finials on concave-front cornice, ribbing along corner panels on front & sides, arched glass panel over white dial w/black Roman numerals & subsidiary seconds dial, the door w/brass lion pull, corner drop finials at base, pendulum bob w/fancy engraved pattern, original No. 1 iron weight, time-only movement, old spliced & glued break on door, lion pull replacement for original lock, ca. 1889, 65" h. **$4,480**

New Haven Spring-Driven Wall Regulator Clock with Oak Case

New Haven: Oak wall regulator, early 1900s, eight-day, time & strike, spring driven, 16" wide, 35" h. $425

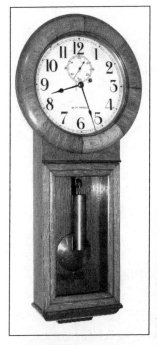

Seth Thomas "Regulator No. 2" Model Wall Regulator Clock with Quarter-Sawn Oak Case and Large Round Molding Surrounding Dial

Thomas, Seth: "Regulator No. 2" model, long quarter-sawn oak case w/large round molding around the white dial w/black Arabic numerals & subsidiary seconds dial, a long rectangular drop case w/glass door w/spring/bullet latch showing the brass weight & pendulum bob, molded base, recabled time-only movement, original dated label on rear shows manufacture by ST division of General Time Corp., wooden bezel has warped & been reglued, ca. 1947, 35 1/2" h. **$896**

*Seth Thomas "Regulator No. 2"
Model Wall Regulator Clock with
Walnut and Mahogany-Veneer
Case, Large Round Molding
Surrounding the Dial, and Glass
Door with Gilt Stenciling*

Thomas, Seth: "Regulator No.
2" model, walnut- & mahogany
veneer-case w/a large round top
molding enclosing the white dial
w/black Roman numerals, long
drop case w/molding at top & bottom, the tall glass door decorated w/a gilt stenciled design of a flying eagle & star within garlanded arch over an oval cartouche & "REGULATOR" all on a black ground, shallow ogee base drop, time-only movement, excellent label inside, ca. 1870, 34" h. **$2,016**

Seth Thomas "Regulator No. 6" Model Wall Regulator Clock with Oak Case and Molded Arched Top with Carved Decoration

Thomas, Seth: "Regulator No. 6" model, long oak case w/molded arched top w/center carved decoration & spike-topped spool corner finials on ogee molding, scroll-carved molding around the original dial w/black Roman numerals, subsidiary seconds dial & brass bezel, tall lower glass pane shows the pendulum & brass bob, short three-quarter round reeded columns w/drop finials at the top & bottom front corners, ogee base drop w/knob drop finial & corner drop finials, hands, weight & case hardware all original, recabled eight-day time-only movement, ca. 1884, 49" h. $4,592

Seth Thomas "Regulator No. 7" Model
Wall Regulator Clock with Walnut
Case, Sunburst Finial, Crest of Scrolls,
and Cornice with Shell Carving

Thomas, Seth: "Regulator No. 7" model, walnut case w/molded out-curved cornice decorated w/shell carving, topped by crest of scrolls curving up at ends & a sunburst finial in center, dial frame w/molding at top & bottom & carved spandrels enclosing a white dial w/brass bezel, black Roman numerals & subsidiary seconds dial, connected to long drop by ribbed & molded band, the drop w/sides that scroll out at top & bottom, a contour frame around glass panel over weight & pendulum, flower-form decorations centered at top & bottom of frame, ribbed molded rectangular base drop suspended from molded base, time-only #62 movement w/cut pinions & maintaining power, some flaking on dial, ca. 1905, 48" h. $12,320

Seth Thomas Short "Regulator No. 8" Model Wall Regulator Clock with Oak Case, Center Molded Arch Crest, and Carved Sunburst Spandrels Around the Dial

Thomas, Seth: Short "Regulator No. 8" model (3" shorter than long version), oak case w/molded pediment & crest w/sides that slant to small scroll ends from center molded arch, the dial frame w/carved sunburst spandrels around the white dial w/brass bezel, black Roman numerals & subsidiary seconds dial, original dial & hands, the bottom section w/contour glass panel showing pendulum, scroll-cut designs at tops of sides, molded base w/small apron & corner drop finials, weight, damascene pendulum, pulley & hardware, No. 62 time-only movement w/dead beat escapement & cut pinions, some wear to dial, pendulum stick may be old replacement, ca. 1905, 52" h. **$9,800**

Seth Thomas "Regulator No. 30" Model Wall Regulator Clock with Oak Case, Shell-Form Crest, and Scalloped Baseboard With Floret

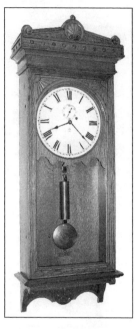

Thomas, Seth: "Regulator No. 30" model, tall golden oak case w/molded pediment topped w/a band of beading under the molded scroll-cornered tapering crestrail centered by a shell-form crest within a circle, reeded molding around the front w/an upper wood panel w/fan-carved upper corners & a scalloped lower border enclosing the large brass bezel & white dial w/black Roman numerals & subsidiary seconds dial, original weight & long pendulum w/damascene brass bob, w/a molded separate shelf w/tapering corner brackets & a scalloped baseboard centered by a floret, 80-beat time-only movement, ca. 1909, 49" h. **$6,160**

Waterbury Clock Company "Regulator No. 9" Model Wall Regulator Clock with Oak Case, Flaring Cornice, and Three Ball Finials Joined by Twisted Brass Rods

Waterbury Clock Company:
"Regulator No. 9" model, very tall oak case w/a high flaring cornice, three ball finials joined by slender twisted brass rods above a flaring gadrooned band over a fan-carved band above a narrow notch-carved band, all above the front frame w/reeded sides & small corner blocks, a tall arched glass panel over the round silvery grey metal dial w/black Roman numerals & subsidiary seconds dial, a single cylindrical brass weight & long pendulum w/large brass bob, the base w/ropetwist border over a scalloped front apron & quarter-round brackets flanking a back panel carved w/a large paterae, solid plate eight-day one-weight time-only movement w/Graham escapement, ca. 1891, 76 1/4" h. **$15,680**

Waterbury Clock Company "Regulator No. 20" Model Wall Regulator Clock with Oak Case and Large Round Molding Surrounding Dial

Waterbury Clock Company: "Regulator No. 20" model, oak case w/a wide round molded top frame around the brass bezel & white dial w/Roman numerals & subsidiary seconds dial, the long base w/a glass door decorated w/a modern "Regulator" decal, pendulum w/large brass bob, rectangular cast-iron weights, time & strike movement, original Waterbury label, beat scale in case bottom, ca. 1905, 38" h. **$1,456**

Welch, Spring & Company "Sembrich" Model Wall Regulator Clock with Walnut Victorian Renaissance Revival-Style Case, Plume Crest, and Scroll-Cut Apron

Welch, Spring & Company: "Sembrich" model, walnut Victorian Renaissance Revival-style case, a large plume crest & scroll ears on the flaring flat cornice over a line-incised frieze above the long rounded glass front over the dial w/Roman numerals, pendulum w/large brass bob, molded base w/slender tapering side brackets above the pointed & scroll-cut, line-incised front apron, eight-day movement, time & strike, refinished case, ca. 1880, 5 1/2 x 14", 39" h. **$700-800**

Glossary

Adamatine: patented colored celluloid applied as a veneer

Advertising clock: clock used for promotional purposes on which the advertising may be found on the case, dial, or tablet

Anniversary clock (a.k.a. 400-day clock): clock that needs to be wound only once a year

Arc: curved path in which the pendulum travels when swinging

Balance: wheel that regulates the rate of movement in clock parts

Banjo clock: clock that roughly resembles a banjo in shape, with a round clock face over a long drop

Barrel: cylinder in a clock that contains the timepiece

Beat: the ticking sound made by the working mechanisms of a clock

Beehive clock: clock with a rounded case that bears some resemblance to a beehive

Bezel: supporting ring that surrounds the dial and holds the glass that covers it in place

Black clock (or Black): clock made of marble, black iron, or black enameled wood, popular from about 1880 to 1920

Blinking eye clock: clock in the form of a human or animal with eyes that blink in time with the beat

Bob: end of a pendulum, generally disc-form

Boulle: tortoiseshell, ivory, and metal inlay on wood

Bracket clock: clock with a specific style of case widely used in eighteenth-century England that sits in a bracket attached to a wall

Calendar clock: clock that indicates the day and month of the year as well as the time

Carriage clock: small portable clock with a handle on top, usually with a brass framework and glass front and side panels

Case: the framework of a clock that contains the working parts

Celluloid: trade name for the first plastic, invented in 1869, that received wide commercial use

Chapter ring: part of the dial that contains the numerals and the marks for minutes and seconds

Cottage clock: a category of inexpensive clocks widely produced in the United States in the late nineteenth century suitable for use in working class homes of the era

Crystal regulator clock: shelf or mantel clock with glass sides, similar to a carriage clock but with a high-quality "regulator" movement

Deadbeat escapement: escapement with no recoil

Escapement: mechanism that regulates the movement of the pendulum or balance wheel

Fusee: grooved cone that equalizes the tension in a spring-driven clock, regulating its speed

Gallery clock: eight-day or electric wall clock, usually round, with a simple case and a dial usually 8 inches or larger for high visibility in a large public area

Gimbal: bracket device, usually seen in ships' clocks, that supports a timepiece and keeps it level

Gothic clock: clock with a pointed case that resembles gothic architecture

Grande sonnerie clock: French term for a clock that repeats the hour strike on the quarter hour

Grandfather clock: tall upright floor clock, also known as a "tall case" clock

Hair-spring: slender hair-like coil that controls the regular movement of the balance wheel in a clock

Horology: science of measuring time or making timepieces

Label: paper inside a clock case that often had not only the name of the manufacturer but also operating instructions and advertisements for the manufacturer

Lantern clock: early clock with a case that resembles an old hand-held lantern

Long-case clock (a.k.a. tall-case clock): another name for a grandfather clock

Lyre clock: variation of a banjo clock with a wood case somewhat resembling a lyre

Mantel clock: clock meant to sit on a shelf or fireplace mantel

Mercury pendulum: cylindrical pendulum with a silvery look made to resemble those in France that originally contained actual mercury

Movement: the mechanism of a clock that produces motion

Novelty clock: clock that performs some movement in addition to keeping time or that is in a form or shape not normally associated with clocks

Number cartouche (a.k.a. signet): separate decorative panel in a dial on which a numeral is painted or attached

Open escapement (a.k.a. visible escapement): the working parts of a timepiece that can be seen through an opening, generally located in the center of the dial

Parlor clock: Victorian clock of the mid-to-late 1800s, with a carved case, often of walnut, that was commonly placed on a mantel or shelf in a parlor

Pediment: ornamental top on a clock case, frequently curved in shape

Pendulum: clock weight, often ornamental, hung from fixed point so as to swing as it regulates a clock's movement

Perpetual clock: calendar clock that automatically adjusts to the variations in the length of months and doesn't need manual adjusting from month to month

Pillar-and-scroll clock: usually attributed to Eli Terry, the style of case popular in the early nineteenth century that features broken scroll pediment and slender round columns

Porcelain or china clock: clock with a case made of glazed porcelain

Regulator clock: usually a large wall clock with a long case enclosing the dial above a long pendulum, noted for its time-keeping accuracy

Reverse painting: decoration painted on the back of a glass panel or tablet

Spandrels: decorations that fill the space in the corners around the chapter ring of a dial

Steeple clock: clock with a Gothic-style case with a peaked top and finials that resembles a church steeple

Strike train: gears that regulate the striking on a time-and-strike clock

Subsidiary dial: small dial incorporated into the main dial that indicates something beyond hours and minutes (i.e. seconds, days of the week, etc.)

Sweep-seconds hand: subsidiary hand that sweeps around the dial, indicating seconds

Swinging-arm clock: timepiece with a standing figure with an upraised arm holding the clock works, with the dial and pendulum forming one long unit that oscillates as the clock beats

Tablet: decorative glass panel on the front of a clock case, frequently reverse-painted or stenciled

Tambour clock (a.k.a. camelback or humpback clock): shelf clock with a case that is flat at each side and rounded in the middle

Time-and-strike: clock that indicates time and strikes the hours or increments of hours with a bell or gong

Tower clock: clock situated in the tower of a public structure

Wagon spring: series of flat springs, used instead of a coil spring to power a clock movement

Wag-on-the-wall clock : a wall clock in which the dial, works, weights, and pendulum are exposed and not contained in case

Weights: in a non-spring-driven clock, heavy objects, usually cylindrical, that power the clock as they drop

Zebrawood (a.k.a. Zebrano): straw-colored African wood with fine stripes that is sliced and used for veneer to cover unattractive wood